K9 SEARCH AND RESCUE TROUBLESHOOTING

K9 Professional Training Series

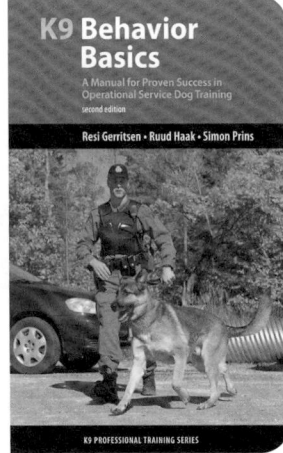

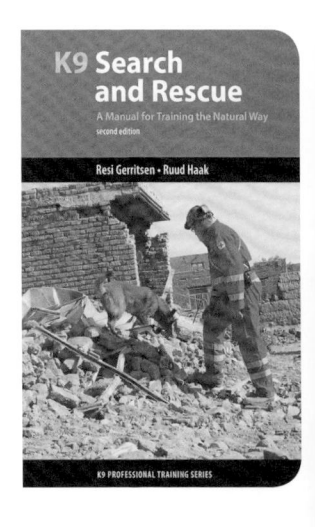

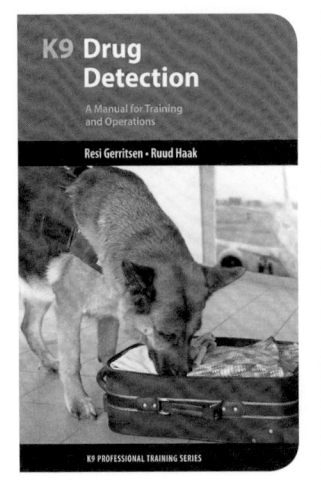

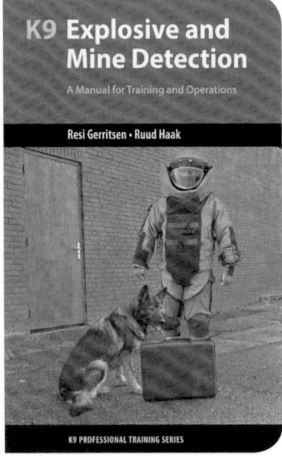

K9 Scent Training — A Manual for Training Your Identification, Tracking and Detection Dog
Resi Gerritsen • Ruud Haak

K9 Behavior Basics — A Manual for Proven Success in Operational Service Dog Training, second edition
Resi Gerritsen • Ruud Haak • Simon Prins

K9 Search and Rescue — A Manual for Training the Natural Way, second edition
Resi Gerritsen • Ruud Haak

K9 Drug Detection — A Manual for Training and Operations
Resi Gerritsen • Ruud Haak

K9 Explosive and Mine Detection — A Manual for Training and Operations
Resi Gerritsen • Ruud Haak

K9 Schutzhund Training — A Manual for IPO Training through Positive Reinforcement, second edition
Resi Gerritsen • Ruud Haak

See the complete list at
dogtrainingpress.com

K9 SEARCH AND RESCUE TROUBLESHOOTING

Practical Solutions to Common Search Dog Training Problems

Susan Bulanda

K9 Professional Training Series

An imprint of
Brush Education Inc.

Copyright © 2017 Susan Bulanda

17 18 19 20 21 5 4 3 2 1

Thank you for buying this book and for not copying, scanning, or distributing any part of it without permission. By respecting the spirit as well as the letter of copyright, you support authors and publishers, allowing them to continue to create and distribute the books you value.

Excerpts from this publication may be reproduced under licence from Access Copyright, or with the express written permission of Brush Education Inc., or under licence from a collective management organization in your territory. All rights are otherwise reserved, and no part of this publication may be reproduced, stored in a retrieval system, or transmitted in any form or by any means, electronic, mechanical, photocopying, digital copying, scanning, recording, or otherwise, except as specifically authorized.

Brush Education Inc.
www.brusheducation.ca
contact@brusheducation.ca

Editorial: Meaghan Craven
Cover Design: John Luckhurst; Cover image: Jim Dobie
Interior Design: Carol Dragich, Dragich Design

Printed and manufactured in Canada

Library and Archives Canada Cataloguing in Publication
Bulanda, Susan, author
K9 search and rescue troubleshooting : practical solutions to common search dog training problems / Susan Bulanda.

(K9 professional training series)

Issued in print and electronic formats.
ISBN 978-1-55059-736-3 (softcover).—ISBN 978-1-55059-737-0 (PDF).—
ISBN 978-1-55059-738-7 (Kindle).—ISBN 978-1-55059-739-4 (EPUB)

1. Search dogs—Training. 2. Rescue dogs—Training. I. Title.
II. Series: K9 professional training series

SF428.73.B84 2017   636.7 0886   C2017-906017-1
                                            C2017-906018-X

Contents

Introduction vii
1 Finding a Good SAR Dog 1
2 Why Dogs Have Training Problems 22
3 What Is Scent? 41
4 The Uncontaminated Scent Article 46
5 Cross Training a Dog 49
6 SAR Dog Training Methods 55
7 SAR Dog Training Problems 58
   Conclusion: Preventing Problems Before They Start 86

Notes 93

Appendix: Following Scent 95

Suggested Resources 104

About the Author 105

Introduction

Over the years, many search and rescue (SAR) dog handlers across North America and Europe have contacted me about training problems with their SAR dogs. Some problems started at the beginning of training and some developed later in the dog's career. Unfortunately, there is no one solution to solving the problems that each dog develops. However, understanding the possible reasons why problems develop and having a few methods at hand to solve them can often work wonders. This book will offer some of the reasons for problems, as well as some solutions.

Although the problems addressed in this book are more common with air-scenting and scent-specific dogs, the solutions apply to all disciplines of SAR work. This is because the basis for the problems is usually the same or similar, regardless of discipline.

Disclaimer

While the contents of this book are based on substantial experience and expertise, working with dogs involves inherent risks, especially in dangerous settings and situations. Anyone using approaches described in this book does so entirely at his or her own risk, and both the author and publisher disclaim any liability for any injuries or other damage that may be sustained.

1

Finding a Good SAR Dog

The selection of a dog to use for SAR is the first step toward developing a successful SAR dog team. By the same token, the wrong dog (or handler) is a recipe for failure. There are three categories of SAR dogs that handlers attempt to train.

Type One: The Pet

When you decide to join a canine SAR team, you typically want to train your pet dog. Often, you entertain notions about you and your dog saving people and being heroes.

If this is you and you are sincere, and your dog is capable and willing, this combination can succeed. However, the first lesson you must learn is that to be a good SAR dog handler, you must first be trained as a rescue person. Then you can specialize in the K9 aspect of SAR. A SAR dog handler is a rescue person who specializes in the use of the K9. The K9 is only one tool a rescue person uses to find missing people, and not all missions require the use of a dog.

Understanding and accepting this key aspect of the SAR dog handler's job is important because it influences your handler mindset, giving the dog a better chance to succeed. If you view

SAR as just another activity for your dog, or a fun thing to do, you will inadvertently communicate that to your dog, which can affect the dog's attitude toward the work. If you do not take SAR work seriously, your dog may not, either. Of course, the dog must enjoy the work and think it is fun. But your attitude toward SAR work should not be the same as when you are playing a game of fetch with your pet. When people have the "It's all a game" attitude, the dog can interpret it to mean, "It is okay if I don't feel like doing it today," or the dog may feel it is acceptable to only do the parts he wants to do. The dog may even feel that if something better comes along, he will do that instead.

As any working dog handler with experience knows, dogs are in tune with the moods and attitudes of the handler, even to the point where they can feel the handler's attitude through the leash. A dog can smell your mood, since our moods change our body chemistry just enough to give a scent signal to a dog. Think of the dog that knows when his owner is afraid and the change in the dog's behavior as a result, or the reaction of the dog when the owner is happy and excited. It is not only the tone of your voice, your body language, and your facial expressions that communicate to the dog, but your scent as well.

Recent studies have shown that dogs have a special area in their brain to process human faces, which gives us another clue as to why dogs are sensitive to human social cues.[1] Dogs are much more aware of what their handlers think, feel, and do than most people give them credit for. Ignorance of or ignoring this aspect of canine/human communication is often at the root of training problems.

From the beginning, therefore, you, the SAR dog handler, must take SAR seriously and leave all ego and romantic notions at home.

Type Two: The Adopted Dog

The second type of dog that handlers use is one they have adopted. While this is a noble idea and can work, it is risky because the adopted dog seldom comes to a new owner with a reliable history. People often lie when they surrender dogs because they believe someone else can fix the dogs' problems, and they want to give the dogs every chance to have a normal life.

Some people believe that by giving up a dog for adoption, the problem will magically go away. Very few dogs are surrendered due to the illness, retirement, divorce, or death of their owners. Most are surrendered because they have behavior problems. Often the original owners of surrendered dogs have created the problems by the way they raised them or did or did not train them, or because they selected the wrong type of dog for their lifestyle and ability to cope with a dog, or simply because they got tired of the dogs. In all cases, the dogs have been short changed and did not get what they needed to succeed.

The people who own dogs with training and/or behavior issues who do not give up on their dogs will seek professional help for their dogs. If that does not work out, they will usually be honest about why they are surrendering them.

Most often a purebred dog that is available for adoption was not purchased from an ethical breeder but came from a commercial breeder or a puppy mill supplier via a pet shop, or from a backyard breeder. This is a reasonable assumption because an ethical breeder will have the puppy buyer sign a contract stating that if the dog does not work out, the dog will be returned to the breeder.

Shelters, of course, also offer mixed breed dogs for adoption. As for what mix a mixed breed is, shelter workers take a wild guess and are often wrong.[2] In some cases, they will see a picture of a rare breed of dog and label the mixed breed as the rare breed or a mix of the rare breed. Most often this is wrong because the rare breeds seldom wind up in a shelter or are bred to a dog that is not the same breed.

DNA tests are a good way to determine what breeds a mix is made of but often are not 100 per cent accurate because there is no record of all the breeds available. However, behaviorists have found that doing DNA tests on mixed-breed or adopted dogs helps them to understand the genetics that influence the way the dogs perceive their world and react to their environment. This can help immensely with the training process.

A dog that has been rescued can work out. Some people have an instinctive ability to pick the dogs that will work. In some cases, the dog surrendered for adoption only needs a job to do, and SAR is a lifesaving experience for the dog.

Mia, a beagle mix, was adopted by Dr. Victoria Barber Emery. Mia was classified as unadoptable but under the care of Dr. Emery, she has improved considerably. This type of dog would not make a good SAR dog but can be a loving pet. (Photo by Dr. Victoria Barber Emery)

Type Three: The Dog from a Breeder

The third type of dog is the one that you, the handler, purposely seek out from a breeder for SAR dog work. Perhaps you are a seasoned handler and have retired or are about to retire your first SAR dog. Often, if your first dog was good, you will look for the same breed or type of dog as the original. Some handlers in this

RETIREMENT

The bond that develops between the SAR, military, or police dog and handler is unique and deep. In many cases, the dog saves lives, even the life of the handler, and the handler may save the dog's life as well.

Handlers learn to read their dogs and the dogs can read their handlers. Often handlers will say that they do not have to tell their dogs what to do—the dogs know. They work together like a professional dance team, moving together in total harmony. Then it must come to an end.

Many years ago, the author did a study about the types of dogs used in SAR work and how long handlers stayed with a unit. Many dog handlers stayed in SAR for about five years. The main reason for this was that after five years their SAR dogs had to retire and they could not bring themselves to train another dog. Keep in mind that if you decide not to train another dog, there are still ways to continue with your unit. There are many jobs in the SAR unit that do not require a dog. The handler's knowledge and experience are still a valuable and needed asset.

Those who do get another dog find it difficult and sometimes frustrating to train and work with the new dog. The old dog worked so well. Often you can recognize the signs of aging and get the next dog to train even as you continue to work with the old dog. It seems that transitioning this way is the least painful way to handle it. It also allows you to assess your new dog to see if he will succeed as a SAR dog and, if not, have time to find one that will work.

It is not unusual for the old SAR dog to become upset when he is left behind on missions or in training. If possible, allow your old dog to work short problems in training and, if he is still able, hasty searches on missions. This will depend on the unit's rules about handling two dogs at the same time. At the least, you should include the old dog in training sessions. It will keep him happy and make him feel included.

situation go to a breeder to get a puppy to train while the first or current dog eases into retirement.

The typical SAR dog works for about five years in the field before retirement looms on the horizon. By the time the dog is seven or older, it is time to retire the dog or limit the size and duration of missions. Some breeds can work longer than others.

The smaller the dog, the longer he can work because his lifespan is longer. For example, the giant breeds, such as Newfoundland, Great Dane, and some large breeds such as the Doberman, live between eight and 10 years, while some medium-sized dogs live from 15 to 18 years and can work up to the age of 10 or 13. The short-lived dogs reach their prime of life shortly after maturity, while the longer-lived breeds have a longer prime of life.

Finding the right dog from the best breeder can be a challenge even if you go back to the breeder who produced your last or current SAR dog. After all, several generations will have passed since your last dog was purchased. The line the breeder currently has will not be the same as before. You may only hope the breeder has not changed breeding goals.

As well, it is possible that the trusted breeder is no longer producing puppies. In that case, you must find a new breeder. One way to start is to ask other handlers who have good dogs where they purchased their dogs. When you have found a good breeder, it is important to conduct an interview with the breeder to further ensure you will end up with a dog that will work.

First and foremost, when you find yourself in this situation, you should only consider a breeder who breeds dogs for work. If the breeder does not specialize in SAR dogs, you should at least ensure that the breeder breeds dogs for field work and not for show. Working dogs are often radically different—in size, coat texture, and temperament, for example—than their conformation show counterparts. If you take a close look at a field-bred English setter, for example, and compare it to a show English setter, you will notice structural differences. The show dog is bigger with a longer top line (back) and the coat is long and fluffy. The field setter has a squarer build, more in proportion, is smaller in size, and has a coarser, shorter coat that is designed to shed dirt and not pick up seeds such as burrs. The show dog is not required to use his brains or instinct for anything but prancing around the ring, while the field dog must prove his hunting ability, stamina, intelligence, and willingness to work to be considered for a breeding program. Many breeders who breed for the show ring believe that function follows form. This is not true as proven by true working dogs. It has only taken a few short years for some breeds to develop a split between those that still retain their working instincts and those that do not.

Choosing a Breed

If you are not sure what breed or type of dog to get, consider the various breeds that have the potential to be good SAR dogs. Often the breeds that are not the most popular are bred truer to the breed characteristics and have fewer health issues since they are not mass produced to meet market demands. I recommend two books to those selecting a breed for SAR work: *Simon & Schuster's Guide to Dogs* (1980) and *The Encyclopedia of Dog Breeds: A Field Guide to 231 Dog Breeds and Varieties* (2011). Both books can be found from used book retailers such as Abebooks.com or Amazon.

Of course, breed books may not tell you everything you need to know about a breed, and breeders are partial to their chosen breed and should be. Veterinarians do not get involved with the temperament and characteristics of breeds in the same way a trainer does. After reading through a breed guide, consider talking to a dog trainer or behavior consultant. They know the characteristics of the breeds the best.

The factors to consider in selecting a breed include:

1. What is the working life span of the dog?
2. What is the breed's coat type and grooming needs? Different climates will dictate what coat type is best, as will the vegetation and terrain features of the areas to be searched.
3. What is the breed's intelligence level?
4. What health issues are associated with the breed?
5. How big is an adult dog? Can you carry your dog out of the field if he is injured? How transportable is the dog?
6. How biddable (willing to obey) is the breed? This is important for a good working dog and ease of training.
7. Is the breed physically able to do the type of work that you want to do?

The individual dog must have good health, a love for people, a safe demeanor with children, the ability to remain calm in stressful situations, and the control required to work off leash, if needed. The dog must not critter/game chase or be nervous, dog aggressive, fearful of strange situations, or aggressive to humans.

When considering which type of dog to get for SAR work, keep in mind that different breeds are interested in different things, which gives each breed its own special set of characteristics. For example, if there is a sheep and a rabbit in a field, a sheep-herding dog will know the rabbit is there but will focus on the sheep. In our parlance, this dog is thinking, "Sheep, sheep, I need to get the sheep. Yes, there is a rabbit, but who cares?" On the other hand, a beagle or other small-game dog will know the sheep is there, but his thought process will run something along

SAR dogs must be safe in all situations, especially around children. The author and search dog Scout, a Beauceron, at a boy scout camp. (Photo by Larry Bulanda)

the lines of, "Rabbit, rabbit, I must get the rabbit. Who cares about the sheep?"

THE STEPS TO CHOOSING A DOG FROM A QUALITY BREEDER

Once you have selected the breed(s) you want to consider, you must find a good breeder and will do well to consider the following guidelines.

KENNEL CLUBS

Contact the United Kennel Club (UKC) or the American Kennel Club (AKC) or the kennel club for your country, such as the Canadian Kennel Club (CKC), and find out if your area has a federation of dog clubs (most states do). Contact the federation for a list of breeders. If the breed you have selected is not registered with your country's national recognized registry (such as the UKC, CKC, or AKC), you can contact the national club for the breed. Some breeds' national clubs have their own registries, such as the Australian Shepherd Club of America or the North American Sheepdog Society. Working-dog registries and clubs, such as the ones listed above, will have breeders dedicated to the working aspect of the breed and are a good place to start.

However, be aware of several unrecognized registries that are designed for puppy mills or are merely clubs that will register anything with fur and feet. I have found that if the breed is a common one and the breeder is not registered with the AKC, UKC, CKC, or a working-dog registry, it is best to avoid it. If you are in doubt, contact the AKC, UKC, CKC, or parent breed club, and ask if the registry in question is recognized by them. If not, it is a hobby registry with no credibility. With a little bit of investigation, you can determine if the registry is a good one or not.

If you decide to import a dog, the breeder's dogs should be registered with the Fédération Cynologique Internationale (FCI), which is the largest worldwide registry in the world. It includes Africa, the Americas, Asia, Europe, the Caribbean, the Middle East, and the Pacific.

After you find breed clubs in your area or breeders through a list from the AKC, UKC, CKC, or the Federation of Dog Clubs, you are ready to make phone calls.

Keep in mind that just because a breeder is listed with one of the organizations does not mean that it is an ethical or "good" breeder. Most state federations require that the breeder sign a code of ethics to be listed in their directories. This is a good start and the first way to filter out the backyard, commercial, and puppy-mill breeders who typically are not involved with any dog-related organization.

Keep in mind that breeders, good or bad, cannot completely control the genetic makeup of the litters they produce. If genetics were an exact science, all dogs would be stellar workers and champions in conformation. A breeder can only try to stack the odds in the dogs' favor.

Although most breeders are not familiar with the Early Neurological Stimulation or Bio-Sensor program for dogs, later known as the Superdog program (originally developed by the US military), it would be ideal to select a dog from a breeder who does employ this program or a similar program.[3] It has been proven to reliably produce mentally and physically healthy dogs.

THE EARLY NEUROLOGICAL STIMULATION PROGRAM FOR DOGS

The Bio-Sensor program, also known as the Superdog program, was developed by the U.S. military to improve performance in working dogs. Through this program, it was discovered that during the first days of life, puppies (and kittens) are sensitive to thermal, tactile, motion, and locomotion stimuli. Follow-up research showed that puppies (and kittens) that received a small amount of stimulation (three to five seconds at a time) administered from the third to 16th days of life benefited later in life.

The person working with the puppies handled them separately and daily, following a certain regimen. The stimulation caused a low level of stress, which is the key to the benefits observed later. Puppies in the program were found to have improved heart rate, stronger heart beats, stronger adrenal glands, more tolerance for stress, and a greater resistance to disease. When tested at an older age, the dogs that had been in the program performed better, were more tolerant of stress and novel situations, were more intelligent, and were overall healthier.

However, the research was not able to determine exactly how many seconds of stimulation each puppy should receive. Some puppies could tolerate more than others. This means it is essential that the person administering stimulation to puppies must be careful not to overdo it, be diligent, and thoroughly understand the process.

INTERVIEW THE BREEDERS

Before you call any of the breeders, prepare a pad of lined paper with a page for each of the breeders you are contacting. On the top of each page, write down the name, phone number, breed of dog, and any other information about the breeder that you want to include. You will use these templates to write down the breeders' answers to the questions that follow. This will help you remember what each breeder says since you may be referred by the breeder to someone else. It is difficult during this process to keep track of who you called and what they had to say if you do not write it all down.

Before you start asking questions of the breeders, identify yourself and tell the breeders how you came to contact them. Explain that you would like to consider their breed of dog as your next SAR dog and that you would like to ask them some questions about their dogs. Keep in mind that good breeders often get many phone calls from prospective puppy buyers, and many people fail to realize that breeders are not stores with unlimited hours of operation and will call at all hours of the day and evening. Be sure to call at a decent time of day or evening and ask if the breeder has time to talk. If it is not a good time, ask when you can call back.

Using your prepared template, write down the answers to the following questions (I provide cues about ideal answers below):

1. How long have you been breeding this breed of dog?

    The longer the better. If they just started, ask if they are being mentored by an experienced person. Breeding is complicated and should not be done by someone who is inexperienced.

2. Do you breed more than one breed of dog? If so what breeds?

    Good, dedicated breeders will only concentrate on one or two breeds. It takes too much time to manage one or two breeds properly to dabble in more. A good working-dog breeder should be competing with dogs in that breed's working competitions. This is the main reason for breeding.

3. Do you belong to a breed club? Which club?

   If not, be suspicious. A breeder with goals needs the support and help of a breed club. Someone who really loves their breed typically wants to interact with like-minded people. The breed club is also a way for the breeder to see how different dogs and lines perform, as well as to discover health issues prevalent in the breed. Breeders who breed for profit do not care as much and are more likely to avoid clubs.

4. Why do you breed dogs?

   The answer should be some variation of "To better the breed."

5. What is your goal when you breed a litter? (This applies to their current litter, planned litter, or past litters.)

   Every breeder should have a goal that improves the breed in a specific way. No vague terms here. The breeder should be able to tell you the traits they are trying to improve or preserve. They should talk more about their adult dogs than the puppies. The breeder should be able to give you a history of their lines and the strong and weak points.

6. How many litters have you bred?

   Someone who has bred multiple litters at once and who produces many litters through "arrangements" is one to be avoided. An example of an arrangement is when a breeder gives a bitch to anyone with the condition that she be bred at least two times and that the breeder gets all or most of the puppies. This means the bitch will be bred whether or not she is worthy of breeding. This also allows the breeder to claim that all their puppies are home-raised, which does not qualify as proper socialization. Often the owner of the bitch in this type of arrangement pays most or all the expenses and does not get a puppy. When the owner has met the contractual requirements, they will breed the bitch again so they can make some money from the dog. With this type of arrangement, it is rare that the bitch or stud have had the tests for genetic health issues common for the breed. An example would be a certification from the Orthopedic Foundation for Animals (OFA) to show that the parents of the litter are free of hip dysplasia, or a certification from the Canine Eye Registration Foundation (CERF) to show that the parents are free of canine eye problems.

7. How many litters do you have at one time?

    You want to pinpoint this information. A breeder who puts their all into a litter cannot do so with many litters at once. You want a breeder who works to support the dogs and does not breed dogs to support themselves.

8. What genetic/physical tests do you conduct on the parents?

    The tests vary from breed to breed. Check with your veterinarian or the breed club to see what tests are necessary for that breed and how likely the breed is to have the defect tested for. For example, certain breeds are likely to have hip dysplasia or elbow problems; these breeds should have both parents rated by the Orthopedic Foundation for Animals with a passable rating before they are bred. If the breed suffers from eye problems, dogs should be examined by a canine ophthalmologist and registered with the Canine Eye Registration Foundation, or if the breed is prone to Von Willebrand's disease, dogs should be tested clear of that. These are just a few of the tests and health issues of which you should be aware. An example of how genetics can affect a dog is demonstrated by a 2017 report showing how German shepherd dogs suffer many health issues due to genetics.[4]

9. How do you prove or justify that a bitch or dog should be bred?

    Every dog that is bred should be worthy to breed. That means the dog should demonstrate mental, temperament, and physical qualities. High intelligence and good temperament are the qualities that make a good SAR dog.

Physical soundness indicates a dog will be healthy and have less chance of incurring vet bills for inherited illnesses. These things are demonstrated by temperament tests, working competitions, and testing for physical issues such as hip dysplasia.

Conformation show wins do not prove anything except that the dog looks good per the breed standard. Always remember that the titles that come after the dog's name (working titles) are more important than the titles before the dog's name (conformation). An example: Am, Can, CH Stardust Parsons Riley, TDX, UD, CGC. The titles in front of the name are breed championships, the titles after the name are working titles. TDX means Tracking Dog Excellent; UD means Utility Dog; and CGC means Canine Good Citizen. In the case of SAR dogs, you want to try to get dogs that have real working titles instead of sport working titles.

10. How do you choose the mate for your dog?

    The mate for a litter should be based on the points in question 9. What you do *not* want to hear is "My neighbor had one so we thought we would breed"; or, "My dog is so good that we wanted one like her"; or, "We wanted to provide quality pets for people."

11. How often do you stud your dog (if you have a stud dog)?

    The dog should not be indiscriminately bred to any bitch that will pay for the service. This shows the owner may not care about the quality they produce. And the owner of the bitch may not care either.

12. What guarantees do you give with a puppy or dog that you sell?

    All breeders should give you some form of a guarantee. At the least, you should be allowed to take the dog to your veterinarian and return the puppy if he is not healthy. The guarantee should explain the terms of a replacement or compensation. Be sure to have any contract reviewed by your lawyer. One of the loopholes that breeders use is to say that they guarantee the puppy for life, but to do this, they require that you return the dog to them knowing that you are not likely to do that. This is how they get out of their guarantee. Also, if you have a dog that develops a serious problem, would you want a dog from the same breeder? (Note: Being required to return a dog because your situation will not allow you to keep it is not the same as a breeder guaranteeing the puppy against health or genetic defects.)

13. Do you have a puppy buyers' contract?

    If they do, they should be willing to mail you one so you can review it. Have your lawyer review it, too. Many problems arise and money is lost over the guarantees noted in puppy buyers' contracts. It is also best to avoid any form of co-ownership. The main purpose for co-ownerships is to allow the breeder to retain breeding and showing rights to the dog.

14. What age do you let the puppies go to the new home?

    All breeds are different. Most puppies should not be released before 12 weeks if the breeder is going to give the puppy the proper socialization. Many let the puppies go at eight weeks. Never take a puppy home earlier than that. A puppy taken from the litter younger than eight weeks is at a high risk of developing behavioral problems. Typically, the breeder who is trying to cut corners will release a puppy at eight weeks of age to save on feeding, care, time, and shots. A truly dedicated breeder will keep the puppy until 12 weeks of age to ensure the puppy gets a good head start. They will also start early training and housebreaking. All puppies need that extra four weeks with the litter and the mother to learn canine social rules. The most important lesson puppies learn from their mother and littermates during this period is bite inhibition.

15. How do you raise the puppy until he goes to his new home?

    You want details about the socialization methods the breeder uses. Be wary of generalizations and statements such as, "We have a lot of kids around to handle the puppies," or, "We have lots of people in and out," or, "This is a busy household." Comments like these imply that the dogs sit and watch the world go by. You want to hear about specific handling and activities the breeder does at each week of age. The ideal breeder will use the Bio-Sensor program with the puppies, especially puppies that are destined for real work such as SAR.[5]

16. How many puppies were in your last litter?

    Be wary if they refuse to tell you. This question is important to act on the next question.

17. Can you give me the names and phone numbers of the people who bought puppies from your last litter?

Socialization includes handling by all types of people. SAR dogs especially must be handled properly by children, such as David Steinke in this photo, so they are comfortable around them. (Photo by Catherine Comden)

Call the owners of the last litter. Ask them what life is like with their new dogs. Listen for statements such as, "He's a great dog except that he barks a lot," or, "This is a great dog but he eats paper." While these idiosyncrasies are not something that the breeder will breed for, they can be inherited tendencies. If five out of seven people say the same thing, there is a chance that this line of dog has these types of idiosyncrasies. Also, ask owners if they would get another dog from this breeder.

Although going through these questions seems like a bit of a chore, you will be amazed at what you can learn about a breeder. After all, you are going to invest a sizable amount of money, time, and heart in your new puppy. While it is impossible to completely predict how a puppy will turn out, by starting with the best you can get, you increase your chances of having your next SAR partner be a stellar search dog.

MEET THE BREEDER

The next step is to meet your chosen breeder and the dogs. You may think you like a breed of dog until you meet one of them. There can be wide variations in one breed of dog. Therefore, you want to be sure the breeder you have chosen has what you like. Visiting the breeder and seeing the breeder's dogs will tell you a lot about the way the breeder takes care of the dogs and the amount of time the breeder spends with them. You do not want a breeder who never works with the dogs or sees them for more than a few minutes a day. You do not want dogs that are raised in kennels, locked in outbuildings, or tied outside houses.

After your visit, contact the breed club and ask about the breeder you like. If necessary, go to a few meetings. A good breeder should be respected by most of the people in the club. If not, find out why. Always get a consensus instead of one person's opinion. If people are hesitant to talk about the breeder, be wary. You will also learn a lot about the different lines of dogs in that breed by talking to the members of the club. If the club's meetings are too far away to attend, at least call and talk to several of the members. Most breeds have local clubs that are part of the national club.

PICKING YOUR PUPPY

Once you have found the breeder and line of dogs you like, let the breeder know you would like to purchase a puppy and then wait for him to be born. Picking out the pup should be easy. If you have a good breeder who produces a good line and consistent litter, the actual puppy selection is not as critical. It is a good idea to let the breeder help match you with a puppy. The breeder should have asked you as many questions as you asked in your breeder interview process. The breeder will have watched the puppies grow and will know which puppies have the best potential for SAR work.

By this time, if you have done your homework and the litter has been born, it is time to pick your puppy. Any young children (even teens) in your family should not have been part of the selection process up until now because they may not understand that the dog is going to be a working dog, not just a pet. Even if they understand this, they may not realize the requirements necessary for a working dog. Therefore, if you have children, they should not yet be present during the selection process.

When the puppies are old enough, eight weeks or older, ask to be in a room alone with them. Stand quietly and let the puppies come to you. Note which one comes first and how that puppy acts toward the other puppies. You do not want the puppy that rushes to you first and leaves you first. This puppy is the bully in the litter. You also do not want the puppy that hangs back.

After the puppies greet you, quietly walk around the room and note which puppy follows you the longest. This is the puppy that will make the best working dog because he is the one most interested in humans. There may be more than one like this in a well-bred, socialized litter. If children are going to be part of the selection process, at this stage choose two or more puppies that are candidates for you.

In your next visit to the breeder, have the breeder only bring out those preselected puppies. Now is the time for your children to be involved in the process; allow them to choose which puppy you bring home. If you only chose one puppy on your last visit, that is okay, and now is the time for the children to meet the new puppy. It is important not to bring your children to your first meeting with the puppies because they may not understand your selection process. Perhaps you decide not to take a puppy at all, and it is difficult enough to walk away from cute puppies that are not right for your situation without having a child crying and begging you to get a puppy. It is also difficult for the child to be disappointed by having to leave the puppies behind.

THE STEPS TO CHOOSING AN ADOPTED DOG

The selection process with adopted dogs is the same in terms of selecting the type/breed of dog you want. If you adopt through a rescue group or a shelter, they should have had a qualified canine behavior consultant evaluate the dog. Be sure to ask about the consultant's credentials. Often people call themselves behavior consultants and they are not.

If the shelter does not have access to a certified behavior consultant, you should find one who will evaluate the dog for you. Remember that the dogs in the shelter have all been given up for a reason. Often the people who surrender dogs are not honest about why they gave the dogs up. They typically love the dogs but cannot deal with their issues. They believe that the next owners will fix the dogs' problems. You must decide if you can face the problems that the dog you have chosen may have and be willing to work with the dog. Keep in mind that some dogs are surrendered because they are aggressive, resource guarders, or otherwise unsafe. If you adopt a dog, you must be willing to take the dog back if you find you cannot correct the issues he may have, or if the dog is a risk to your family or is not interested in SAR work. Of course, the adopted dog can still be part of your family if someone else in your house is willing to take on his training and care while you train a new dog for SAR work and then leave on missions.

If you plan to adopt a purebred dog, ask breeders or a veterinarian about the health issues associated with the breed. Breeders are often more up-to-date on health issues than veterinarians, who must know about health issues for all dogs.

Adopted dogs typically need three to six months to adjust. Their personalities and behavior issues may not surface until they settle in. They may become better or worse, but they rarely stay the same. However, many adopted dogs turn out wonderfully, can do SAR work, and certainly deserve a forever home.

2

Why Dogs Have Training Problems

The Trainer

Sometimes dogs' training and behavior problems begin with their trainers. Most SAR units have a head trainer. Unfortunately, very few are professional or experienced dog trainers. Methods for training have often been passed down to the trainer from the previous senior person, who in turn received her training from the last "head trainer." Alternatively, the trainers try to teach the dogs in the unit after reading a dog-training book.

Books can be a wonderful guide for someone who understands the principles of dog training, but nothing can replace hands-on learning. Think of it like this: if an auto mechanic understands the basics of an engine and the components of a car, the mechanic will be able to use the manuals specific to different models and types of vehicles to learn about details unique to each vehicle. But if someone who does not understand car engines or how to use the equipment were to try to fix a vehicle, it would be next to impossible unless that person also received training.

Trying to train a variety of dogs without understanding how dogs learn, what methods are available, and the various instincts for each type of dog is likewise almost impossible. Different individual dogs as well as different breeds learn differently. Therefore, no one method fits all dogs. Often the method needs to be adjusted slightly for the dog so she can understand what is expected of her, or the method of communication must be altered. However, there is never a need to use harsh, outdated methods or any type of punishment.

The other element that trainers often overlook is the handler. If the handler does not understand what to do and the trainer cannot explain it to the handler, the dog will not succeed.

Therefore, the head trainer of K9 SAR units must be dog trainers *and* teachers. They do not have to be paid professionals, but they should at least have training and have worked with a variety of dogs before they attempt to train SAR dogs.

TRAINING OPTIONS

There are several ways you, the potential SAR dog trainer, can undergo training and get experience working with dogs. You could join a dog-training organization that offers courses on how to be a dog trainer, or you could find a trainer who will act as a mentor. This may be difficult to do because dog trainers are often competitive and may be concerned that the people they teach will end up competing with them for business.

Taking several dogs through an obedience program is another way to start learning how to be a dog trainer. Once you get a handle on the methods and steps needed to teach a dog basic obedience or even tricks, you can volunteer at a local shelter or rescue center, where you can practice on as many types of dogs as you can. Although this will take time, it is no different than getting the training you need to pass your SAR certifications. Ultimately, both handlers and head trainers need this type of instruction and practice to enable the dogs in their unit to pass their certifications.

It is important to take potential SAR dogs into various surroundings to get them accustomed to all environments. Here a young flat-coated retriever, Hattie, is practicing obedience in the city with her handler, Linda Spangler. (Photo by Ann McGloon)

THE KEY TO TROUBLESHOOTING: DIAGNOSIS

The mistake that most SAR dog handlers and trainers make is to use the same training methods they initially used when they trained a dog to try to correct a problem with that same dog's performance. If the initial method did not work, it will not work to correct the problem that it caused to begin with. If you as the head trainer understand the nuances of dog behavior and training, you can often fix the training problem. But you cannot do this if you do not understand how to train a dog. The most important role a head trainer has involves diagnosing why dogs in their care are having problems. Fixing the problem is often easy if you understand what the problem is. Diagnosing the problem is the difficult part. Most problems stem from a combination of dog and handler mistakes.

Ideally, the unit should have more than one dog trainer to provide backup and team effort. Learning to be a dog trainer is both interesting and fun. In addition to the needed expertise you can impart to your unit as a trainer, think about the money you could help the unit raise—and the service you could provide to other units and perhaps the public—by offering occasional puppy or basic obedience classes

The Dog

A small portion of problems that arise in training the SAR dog are due to the dog's genetics, personality, and past experiences. Most dog training books fail to explain that individual dogs, like people, have likes and dislikes. Even if a dog is bred to do a certain task, there are members of that breed that are not interested in working.

A good SAR dog trainer understands that dogs pay attention to different things than humans do. Often, what is important to a human is of no interest to a dog, and what the dog finds interesting, most humans are not aware of. For example, you can go for a walk in the park and when you come home your dog will greet you the same as he always does. But if you stopped at a zoo or petted another dog, your dog will examine you thoroughly when you walk through the front door. This is because your dog is interested in the scents you are carrying. However, experience can teach a dog to be interested in something he normally would not pay attention to. For example, if a dog learns that riding in a vehicle means something pleasurable at the end, he will love to ride in a vehicle. However, as some dog owners have learned, if the ride always ends up at a place the dog finds unpleasant, such as the veterinarian, groomer, or kennel, the dog will dread riding in a vehicle.

It is also important to realize that due to the popularity of some breeds, the working instinct has been bred out of them completely or almost completely. It takes only three generations of poor breeding for a breed to lose its keen working instincts.

The saving grace is that most all dogs still have some degree of a hunting instinct. If the breed or type of dog you have chosen has lost its breed-specific instincts, the dog may be able to be trained

A good SAR dog has a balance of drive, instincts, and biddability. Nakita, a Labrador retriever, in the field. (Photo by Jim Dobie)

if he has enough general dog hunting instincts (also known as prey drive). It is the hunting instinct that gives the dog his drive to find things. Satisfying this instinct is rewarding for him. But again, the strength of this instinct can vary from individual to individual. It is important to keep in mind that what the dog wants to hunt or find can vary, as well. Some dogs will go nuts for critters and not care about humans and vice versa.

The dog's problems or successes in training depend on two major things: genetics and handling in early life. There is no doubt that genetics play a huge role. You can have two dogs from the same litter and one will be bold and confident and the other fearful and timid.

Puppies from the same litter can react differently to the same socialization and handling due to individual personalities and/ or different genetics. The puppies from the same litter could be a variety of mixed breeds, or even if they appear to be all purebred, they can still have different sires, which means their genetic makeup is different. (Females ovulate at different times over a period of weeks, and one sperm fertilizes one egg. During this time, she can be bred by any number of males.)

Puppies go through both physical and mental stages of development, the same as people. The main difference is that they go through these stages in a drastically shorter period. A good trainer understands that puppies deal with specific stimuli best at certain stages. By understanding the stages and the effect they have on the mental development of the puppy, the trainer/handler will be able to determine the causes of some problems.

Knowing the causes will help the trainer develop a training program to overcome the problems or perhaps make the decision to retire the dog from a training program.

STAGES OF DEVELOPMENT

THREE TO FOUR WEEKS

The puppies start to follow each other. They become aware that other puppies are in the litter. While they cuddled and slept next to their littermates before this, they were not likely thinking about those other bodies as other puppies.

THREE TO EIGHT WEEKS

The puppies learn to interact with other dogs. This is important for their social development and where they learn their manners. Dogs that are denied safe interaction with other puppies and their mother at this time often lack the canine manners necessary to get along with other dogs.

FOUR TO 10 WEEKS

This is the best time for overall socialization. Puppies that are raised in poor conditions and are sold to pet shops at five to six weeks of age suffer mentally and socially for the rest of their lives, as do puppies that are kept in raised cages or barns and forced to fight for their food because one food dish is given to the whole litter. The result of these conditions is often resource guarding,

Puppies must be allowed to stay with the litter, ideally until 12 weeks of age, to learn how to interact properly. A litter of English shepherd puppies. (Photo by Catherine Comden)

shyness, aggression, separation anxiety, or the inability to bond with humans.

Five Weeks: Puppies will rush toward a new stimulus. This is when well-bred puppies that have solid temperaments have a zest for life and curiosity that enables them to explore.

Five to Seven Weeks: This is the best time for handling by humans. The puppies have not developed fears and if they do not have a poor temperament, they will start to bond with humans. Handling at this time should include people other than the breeder and the breeder's immediate family.

Five to Nine Weeks: This is the best time to introduce leashes, head halters, collars, and any other equipment, such as seat belts, muzzles, and harnesses. All equipment must be introduced in a non-threatening manner.

Six to Seven Weeks: Separation from companions and familiar environment has the most severe effect on puppies at this age.

Socialization is important for puppies between the ages of four and 10 weeks. Puppies need to interact with people. Jonathan Steinke and the pup, Jordy. (Photo by Catherine Comden)

Therefore, puppies placed in new situations at this age have many behavioral problems. Stress at this stage of development will hinder a pup's ability to learn for the rest of his life. This is probably one of the major reasons why puppies raised in puppy mills and by backyard and commercial breeders have many behavior problems. Puppies taken from their mother at six weeks of age are more likely to be developmentally delayed, both mentally and physically. Taking pups away from their mother at six weeks does not make them bond better to humans. Instead, this is the time when puppies in a litter form a pack, allowing them to practice their manners and

When the puppy is between five and nine weeks old, introduce training equipment such as head harnesses. Jordy tries out his head harness. (Photo by Catherine Comden)

learn to interact with each other. This is the time when they learn bite inhibition, which is best taught by littermates and Mother.

FIVE TO 12 WEEKS

This is the optimum time for puppies to learn about people outside the breeder's family. All contact must be non-threatening and fun. This is also the time gentle puppy training can start. The breeder should be working with the puppies to get them used to being handled.

16 TO 20 WEEKS

During this period, puppies do best with novel situations. This is when it is ideal to take the puppy out into the world, if it is done carefully and gradually. For example, you should not take your puppy near heavy construction work or a gun range now to get him used to these sounds. The puppy can hear the noise from a distance, and as he gets older and used to the noise, you can gradually take him closer and closer to the source. However, you should introduce puppies born and raised in rural or quiet suburban neighborhoods to the noises of the city. This must be done gradually in a fun manner.

Too much stress introduced too early in life decreases the dog's ability to learn. Dogs that are isolated from three days to 20 weeks of life cannot adjust to life normally. Judging what too much stress is for each puppy requires close observation, a critical eye, and experience. It will vary from pup to pup.

All puppies go through a "fright stage." Some puppies or young dogs do not handle novel situations very well when in the fright stage. However, if properly handled, they pass through this stage without lasting effects. Many dogs go through this stage at about eight weeks of age, but some as late as nine months. The worst thing you can do if your puppy/young dog shows fear during this stage is make a fuss over the dog, which only calls attention to the fear. In addition, the act of trying to comfort the dog is almost always interpreted by the dog as approval and praise for being frightened. The best way to handle fears at this stage is ignore your dog's behavior and the source of the fear, and leave the area quietly.

Play behavior is critical for the well-rounded development of the puppy/young dog, especially if he is going to be a SAR dog and must get along with other dogs in the unit. To sum it up, play is one of the most powerful activities that shape a dog's behavior and provide social outlets. Play allows a dog to learn how to behave with other dogs, as well as other species, in a safe and acceptable manner. Dogs that are shipped and sold through outlets are often denied the opportunity to interact with other puppies.

If you are not sure if your puppy has had the opportunity to play with other puppies, enroll him in a puppy kindergarten class immediately. At the least, arrange play dates with other puppies. Interaction with an older dog should only be allowed if there is no doubt that the older dog is good with puppies.

Young flat-coated retriever Hattie, practicing obedience in the city with handler Linda Spangler. (Photo by Ann McGloon)

The author's Beauceron, Scout, as a puppy, becoming familiar with future search environments.

Play behavior and activities:

1. Stimulate group behavior,
2. Allow social interaction,
3. Teach puppies correct adult behavior during the "safe" period (before puberty when adult dogs allow silly

behavior from puppies that they might not tolerate from another adult dog. Puppies are more willing to tolerate rough behavior from each other),
4. Develop social relationships,
5. Develop physical and mental dexterity,
6. Refine physical coordination,
7. Allow puppies to experiment with behaviors and develop ritualized behaviors,
8. Allow puppies to learn social rules,
9. Encourage exploration of the environment, and
10. Provide an outlet for complex problem solving.

You must be careful with your puppy during play dates and socialization encounters. Puppies that experience bullying or hard biting during puppyhood or play times will suffer later in life.

Play behavior is critical for puppies. Play should include other puppies and older dogs. Lizzie and her puppy, Annabelle, Cavalier King Charles spaniels. (Photo by Catherine Comden)

They often do not get along with strange dogs, and they tend not to play with toys.

If you, the handler, spot a behavior problem in a young puppy, it is most likely genetically caused. This is especially true if you obtained the puppy at or before 12 weeks of age and noticed a problem by the time the dog reached six months of age. Puppies should not exhibit aggression, nastiness, resource guarding, excessive boldness (all puppies should startle at sudden noises—what counts is the recovery time, which should not take more than a few minutes), fighting with other puppies/dogs, or intolerance for any class of humans (i.e., children, males, females, the elderly). Even breeds that are bred to behave antisocially should not fully exhibit these behaviors at a young age.

If your SAR puppy shows any unacceptable behavior, it may be best to exchange the puppy for one that does not exhibit these behaviors. Typically, a SAR dog handler does not have the knowledge or time to work with a puppy to resolve these issues, which must be eradicated before he can be a safe SAR dog.

If the problem is a result of the dog's genetics, it is important to understand that genetics cannot be changed and will have a strong influence on your puppy for the rest of his life. A severe traumatic event can also result in behavior problems that can last the rest of the dog's life. If you decide to rehabilitate a problematic puppy, do so with the help of a certified canine behavior consultant. You can find one through the International Association of Animal Behavior Consultants (www.iaabc.org). Although a handler may help a puppy overcome a traumatic experience, given the right circumstances the adult dog may react with the original behavior. Dogs never forget.

Communication with the Dog

If the dog is well balanced and does not have behavior/training issues, most training problems are a result of miscommunication between the dog and the handler/trainer. There are five important concepts you must understand when working with your dog.

1. Dogs do not understand *intentions*. They only know what you show them.
2. Dogs can learn concepts if they are taught properly in a step-by-step manner. Reverse chaining builds concepts. A concept is a collection of ideas that help the dog understand something they might not have imagined previously. For example, in water-search training, a dog must learn that he cannot run across water, that it is not solid. Next, he must understand that things can be in the water that he cannot see. By being allowed to wade into water, he learns that water is not solid. By watching a diver enter the water and disappear, he learns that things can be in the water that he cannot see. Then by associating the scent of a human that rises to the surface of the water and then (in training) being rewarded for finding the scent and

REVERSE CHAINING

Reverse chaining is a proven method for training a dog to follow multiple steps. The trainer/handler begins by teaching the final step and then works backward through the steps. When the dog understands what the goal of the exercise is, he can learn to perform the necessary steps to attain that goal. It is impossible to communicate to a dog what the goal is if the trainer tries to teach the dog from step one. The dog may think that each step is an entity unto itself and not the beginning of a series of steps that lead to a goal.

Search training uses reverse chaining to teach a dog to find the object of the search. An example is air scenting. The first step in training is to let the dog see the volunteer hide and, when the dog's excitement is high, to let the dog run to the volunteer. The dog learns to run to the volunteer with the initial runaway. The goal is to find the person. Gradually the dog must look harder and in different circumstances to achieve the goal: finding the missing person.

Reverse chaining can be used to train a dog any exercise that has multiple steps.

seeing the diver appear, he connects the concept with land searching (presumably he was trained to find people on land first). It is ideal to train your dog to air scent before training him to search in water.
3. Only teach a dog one thing at a time, and break it down into the smallest pieces.
4. Nothing works all the time, and everything works some of the time. Understanding this will answer most of the questions handlers have about training.
5. The cause of many training and miscommunication issues between dog and handler arise when a handler does the same thing over and over and expects different results.

UNDERSTANDING THE MIND OF THE DOG

Many dog handlers do not understand the mind of a dog, which leads them to believe in and employ outdated concepts and training methods. Scientists are learning all the time about how dogs think and feel. What they have proven so far creates a radically different picture of the dog's mind than was previously thought.

Many of the older training methods assumed that dogs are no more than tame wolves and used wolf studies as a base. Advanced DNA studies have shown that dogs are not tamed or domesticated wolves; scientists think dogs are a whole different branch from wolves.[1] Some older training methods are based on ideas that have been proven to be detrimental to a dog's physical and mental well-being.

Just a few of the most recent studies at the time of this writing have shown that dogs can be optimists or pessimists,[2] they recognize the smile on your face,[3] and they can follow your gaze.[4] Knowing these facts (and more) about dogs helps you recognize and understand how to train your dog.

Dogs communicate mostly through body language, which includes full body movement, facial expressions, and spatial control

Larry Bulanda and border collie Jib, becoming familiar with a helicopter.

SAR dogs must be introduced to and feel comfortable with water. Doberman pinscher Retta is owned and trained by Michelle L. Limoges, Search and Rescue Dog Association of Alberta, Canada, (SARDAA). (Photo by Sue Hall)

or lack of it. Along with body language, dogs use their sense of feeling, smell, hearing, and sight. Sight is the least useful of the senses to a dog. They will trust in the information their other senses provide before that provided by sight. The degree to which dogs do this varies from individual to individual. All dogs function basically the same when it comes to communication.

One thing that hinders some dogs, causing them to misinterpret signals, is facial hair. Dogs have a wider field of peripheral

An older dog can sometimes help a younger dog explore new environments like a lake. Weimaraner puppy Seagram, and Labrador retriever Soba. (Photo by Catherine Comden)

It is important to show a dog that people and things can be in the water. Ann McGloon's Sussex spaniel, Beryl, and diver Neil Sager with the Josephine County Dive Team. (Photo by Lynda Spangler)

vision and a lesser range of binocular vision than humans. This means that hair on the side of their faces (and hair in front of their faces) blocks their view. Many dogs startle or become afraid and show fear and aggression because they cannot see well. It is essential for the SAR dog to have no facial hair that in any way blocks his field of vision.

Research has shown that the dog is the most capable of understanding humans of a variety of animals tested, including chimpanzees. For example, dogs understand what humans mean when they point at something.[5] They understand that they are being directed to pay attention to the area pointed at. While this can be a useful tool in training the SAR dog, it can also be the undoing of some aspects of SAR dog training, which I will explain later.

When handlers are not also dog trainers or under the guidance of a dog trainer, they will not understand how human body language can show a dog the wrong thing in training. This causes misunderstanding between what the handler wants and what the dog learns because the dog will believe the body language of the handler first.

It is reasonable to say that every dog owner at one time or another has said one thing with the voice and the opposite with the body, causing the dog to be confused. For example, bending over to kiss and hug your dog while putting your arm around his neck communicates two very different things to him. Bending over a dog is considered a threat for many dogs, putting your arm around the dog's neck is a gesture of dominance and threatening behavior. Even though your voice may be soothing, your body is not. Kissing a dog around the face signals submission. So, in dog language, the act of bending over, cooing, and hugging your dog says that you are threatening, submitting, and challenging the dog all at once. How the dog reacts to this will depend on his temperament, age, training, relationship with humans, and experience.

Behavior and training problems, as well as successes, are determined by genetics, which are controlled by your dog's breed or type, how he is raised by the breeder, how he is handled and trained by you, and his general experiences in life. They are also a result of proper communication between the dog and you, his handler.

3

What Is Scent?

To properly train SAR dogs, you must understand what scent is, how dogs detect it, and what they detect.

Scent is composed of microscopic particles, oils, and gases that come from the scent source. We all have experienced both pleasant and unpleasant aromas and odors. Magnify these a trillion times and that is what a dog can detect—one part per trillion.

To try to put it into perspective, if you take one gram of butyric acid (a substance that is released in human perspiration), which is one drop from an eyedropper, and release it in a 10-story building, a person could smell it where it is released only at the moment when it is released. A dog, however, can smell the same amount of acid throughout a fair-sized city even up to 300 feet from the ground. That would be over and above the normal city smells.

Put another way, if you bake a cake, you can smell the whole cake. A dog, however, can smell each ingredient in the cake, the lingering aromas from the oven that cling to the cake, your scent from handling the cake and cake pan, as well as any other scents that might be in the air in your house and that might fall on the cake.

The Dog's Scent Picture

It is beyond our ability to imagine how things smell to dogs. They live in a world of scent and have a unique ability to sort the different scents and understand what they mean. As a result, we can successfully train them to look for particular scents.

But what do they follow? What is a dog's scent picture? The first thing you, the trainer or handler, must understand is that no human can answer these questions. Some people feel that dogs follow crushed vegetation. This theory is an old one and accepted by many dog trainers. However, if this were true, dogs would not be able to detect the scent they are trained to find in water or over hard surfaces such as parking lots, or over frozen ground. And they can do all those things. Recent research has shown that dogs do follow scent and not crushed vegetation.[1]

Many handlers know that dogs detect the skin cells that fall from a human body. This has been proven to be a major source of scent for a dog. For many years, dogs have been taught to identify people out of a lineup, matching one of the people to a scent that was stored on a gauze pad, taken from a weapon used in a crime. The sources for this kind of scent are skin cells and body oils.

We know each person has a unique, individual scent and a family scent. The elements that make up these scents are varied. During the Vietnam War, US soldiers learned that the Vietnamese could smell them before they could hear or see them. The Vietnamese were detecting the grooming products the foreign soldiers used—deodorant, shampoo, aftershave lotion, and so on.

Our individual scent picture as well as our family scent is made of all the products we use in our homes. It is also a result of the food we eat, the clothes we wear, any pets we have in our homes, and livestock we have outdoors. It includes the vegetation that grows around our houses or that we encounter daily. Our scent incorporates the places we have been to, such as the supermarket.

WHAT IS SCENT?

This explains why our dogs give us the once over after we have visited or handled other animals.

Just as we do not pay attention to all the sights and sounds we encounter daily, neither do dogs pay attention to everything they can smell or hear. They block out the usual and common just as we do. When something is different, it catches their attention just as it does for us. Therefore, a dog will react to the track of a person in a field that otherwise has no human scent. This does not mean, however, that a dog cannot follow the track of a specific person in a field full of other human scents.

It is also important to understand that a dog that is following scent is also using her eyes and ears. Many people forget about this

Scent-specific dogs need to be enthusiastic and focused. Young bloodhound Annie is an excellent example of a working bloodhound, handled by Sue Fleming, former president of the National Search Dog Alliance. (Photo by Adriana Pavlinovic)

and feel that a dog only follows her nose. A dog may see disturbed soil, and will note terrain features and wind direction. Recent studies show that animals in general use their whiskers to determine wind direction.[2] All the dog's senses help her analyze the scent she is either looking for or following.

The SAR dog handler must never forget that scent is very important to dogs. Just as we live in a visual world, dogs live in a scent world. To get a glimmer of how important scent is to a dog, think of how much a person is influenced by scent. Think of all the companies that try to make their products more appealing to us by adding specific scents. Just as certain scents appeal to certain people, it is reasonable to assume that certain scents appeal to certain dogs. This is evident in the dogs bred to follow a specific type of game.

Affects on Scent

Understanding what makes up scent, however, is only half of what you need to understand about your dog's olfactory capabilities. To successfully train or work a SAR dog, it is critical that you, the handler, understands how the wind, weather, and terrain affect scent. The best scent dog cannot detect scent if it is not there. If you understand how scent travels, you can use your dog to the best advantage. Keep in mind that a dog can only tell you if there is scent or not. An experienced dog can learn how to work the wind to find scent but she does not understand the rest of the picture. It is up to you to help your dog search in the areas where the scent will most likely be.[3] The illustrations in the Appendix of this book, starting on page 95, provide an overview of scent movements you need to know for land and water rescues.

One way to learn how scent moves is to use the small round smoke bombs available in most discount stores or online. After your dog has worked out a problem, place the smoke bomb where the subject was hidden and watch how the smoke travels. This will show you where the scent traveled and help you understand why your dog did what she did. The smoke bombs have an odor that most people can detect, which can also help you understand what your dog detected. In some cases, for a training exercise, SAR units buy larger smoke bombs and place them in different settings to show how weather conditions affect scent and how scent travels. This is a very valuable lesson for you, the handler, and the easiest way to learn how scent travels in different conditions.

4

The Uncontaminated Scent Article

Most SAR dog handlers insist that their dogs require an uncontaminated scent article to do their work. Considering what makes up scent, is there such a thing as an uncontaminated scent article? The answer is a firm no. Picking up a scent article with a pen, pencil, or other object does not stop your own scent from falling on the object. In fact, your scent is likely already on the pen or pencil you used to pick the object up with. This is because your skin cells and body gases (breath) have fallen on the article. If the article was collected in a missing person's home, that person's family scent is on it, as well as the scent of every living thing in the home and every recent visitor to the home, not to mention every scent that was carried on the breeze while the article was being transported, and/or the scent that was in the container the article was put into. (Remember: one part per trillion!) The odor of the scent article is also made up of its composition, such as cotton for cloth or petroleum products for a synthetic fabric, the dye used to color it, and any other chemicals used in the fabrication of the material. It also includes the products it is washed in: detergent, fabric softener, and the type of water in the household. There is a big difference between the smells of different types of water, such as well water, city water, or untreated water.

However, most of the scents that make up the "uncontaminated" scent article are common, and dogs do not seem to pay attention to them. When you have a scent article that is unique to one person, that person's scent stands out. Therefore, you can teach your dog to identify the scent of the person. By carefully using a scent article that is replete with that person's scent (so, that scent overrides all the others), you can communicate to your dog that he is to follow that scent. Other weaker but more unique scents that are on the article make up the whole scent picture. This scent picture can vary from item to item, location to location, and with the passing of time. This is important to understand since it can be an element that causes training problems. Since we do not know exactly what the dog detects or how the dog relates the scent picture to the item or person he is asked to look for, it is critical in training that you teach the dog to follow the strongest human scent on an article. It is also critical that you, the handler, are sure that the right scent is on the article when training your dog.

Understanding what scent is and how it moves helps you realize and understand that one of the most damaging things a handler can do is re-command a dog while he is following a scent. This is especially counter-productive when training and working a dog that is new to scent discrimination and causes more dogs to fail than anything else. Here is what usually happens. The handler will give the dog the scent article, either an object or a footprint, and command the dog to find that person. (This is assuming the dog has already been trained to follow a handler-identified scent.) As the dog works, he may need to slow down or stop to evaluate the scent picture because, unbeknownst to the handler, another person has walked across the trail or the scent from a person nearby blew onto the trail, or the scent is no longer low but high. At this point, the handler may point to the ground, and re-command the dog to follow the scent. Up to now, the dog has been taught that the handler points to the scent source he is to follow. So, the dog may think that he is to follow a new scent. If the dog does this and the handler realizes that the dog is not following the original scent, the handler will typically think that the dog has lost it or is not trained well, when in fact the dog is doing exactly what he was taught to do. This situation causes the handler to lose faith in the dog when in fact the dog was only doing what he was told. A newly trained dog will not be able to figure out that it is handler error. This scenario can untrain the dog and/or cause the dog to become unreliable, or make it difficult or impossible for the dog to learn the correct thing to do.

Issuing a different command that encourages your dog to keep working is not the same as re-commanding your dog to follow a specific scent. It is best to say nothing to the dog and let the dog indicate he is working it out, has lost the scent, or has stopped working for another reason. For example, would you want your dog to forge ahead on a trail when he realizes there is danger ahead? The dog should have the freedom and experience to be able to communicate what he knows to you, his handler.

5

Cross Training a Dog

For years, there have been many debates over a person's ability to cross train a dog. Some people say no and others say yes, and they are both adamant in their opinions.

Let's look at what cross training means for the dog. She must understand the differences in various situations and follow the rules established by her handler regarding techniques to apply in the given situation.

Consider the guide dog for the blind. Her job is to keep her handler safe from objects and situations. Of course, the dog cannot be trained for each and every possibility, but she must constantly be deciding what to do: stop, turn around, go left or right, or proceed when it is safe to move forward.

The SAR dog knows the object of all training is to find human scent. That scent may be on land, in water, in rubble, or in the ground. The dog can make further distinctions, depending on whether the scent is alive or dead, a general scent or a specific scent. Even without training, the dog knows the differences in scent. All you as the trainer or handler must do is label those differences to identify which one your dog must look for and give her the means to communicate what she knows to you.

In another example, an air-scenting dog must know how to quarter her sector and look for any human scent in the area. The scent-specific dog must understand that she is following one scent that was identified by her handler.

A human remains detection (HRD) dog must work an area differently, depending on if she is working a water search, land search, or disaster search. However, the scent she is looking for is the same. The way different dogs work a search and the signals they give may vary.

Can dogs make the necessary distinctions between scenarios and not mix up the different situations? Many dogs can do this easily. Why, then, are there two camps on the issue of cross training? Often it comes down to how people feel a dog thinks and what opinion they have of the dog's ability to reason. Also, people who are not qualified dog trainers have tried to cross train dogs unsuccessfully, so their opinion is colored by that experience. Finally, some dogs are simply unable to grasp the concept, but we cannot know for certain if the problem resides with the dog or her trainer.

Dogs, like people, have various degrees of intelligence. While certain breeds have reputations for being very intelligent, it always comes down to the individual dog. Dogs can range from highly intelligent and biddable to not-so-bright but willing. Some are intelligent but with an attitude of "I'll do it when I feel like it."

To be cross trained, the dog must be highly intelligent and willing to do what she is told—in other words, she must be biddable. This requires a strong ability on the dog's part to exercise self-control. After all, obedience for a dog is not a matter of knowing what to do or not do, but the ability to exercise self-control to do what she is told as opposed to doing what she wants. Consider the dog with excellent search ability that can perform wonders in the field, until a deer crosses her path and she cannot exercise the self-control needed to stay to task and not chase the deer.

CROSS TRAINING A DOG

Larry Bulanda's border collie, Ness, cross trained in air scenting, scent specific, HRD land and water, disaster live and deceased, and sheep herding.

The author and her Beauceron, Scout, searching for missing divers in Dyers Quarry, Pennsylvania. Scout was cross trained in air scenting, scent specific, HRD land and water, disaster live and deceased, and sheep herding.

Larry Bulanda and Scout doing scent-specific training.

The author and Scout looking for a subject missing in a flood.

The decision of whether or not to cross train a dog is best made before SAR training starts. This is because dogs follow a natural progression when seeking a scent, no matter what they are looking for.

They will first air scent, looking for the general area where the object is located. An example is the bird dog that quarters the field, looking for the scent of a bird. Once the bird dog locates the general area of the scent (the scent cone), she will put her nose where the scent is strongest and follow it. At this point the dog is following a specific scent of an individual bird. Next, she will follow the track of the bird until she gets close enough to pick up the concentrated scent of the bird hiding in brush. The dog will not be distracted by other animal scents or even other bird scents once she is on a hot track. The air-scenting SAR dog does the same. If the hidden person's scent started off airborne, but the dog finds a hotter scent of the hidden person on the ground, she will follow it with her nose down.

Therefore, it is natural to train the dog to air scent first and then do scent-specific work next. When you follow this progression, the training will feel natural for your dog and, if done properly, will build her drive to find people.

All other training can easily follow air-scent work. The advantage to cross training a dog is that the dog can perform in any given situation on a mission. In many cases, a unit will not have enough qualified dogs to have a dog for each discipline. Even if it does, there is no guarantee that those dogs will be available for each mission.

Dogs will not make mistakes if they are cross trained properly. Many units and handlers feel that dogs may get confused and make mistakes on a mission. Dogs are much smarter than we give them credit for.

The secret to cross training a dog is communication. Each discipline must have its own command and alert. Once that is

The author's border collie, Jib, was trained in air scenting, scent specific, disaster live and deceased, HRD land and water, and detection of toxic mold in sick buildings.

established, the dog will fully understand what to do and how to communicate what she has found to you. The only signal that can be consistent in all disciplines is the "all clear" signal, the signal that the dog gives when the object she was asked to search for is not in the area. Teaching an "all clear" signal will avoid false alerts.

With the right dog and a good trainer, a SAR dog can be cross trained to do jobs other than SAR. The author's Beauceron, Scout, and her husband Larry's border collie, Ness, were trained in air scenting, scent specific, HRD land and water, disaster live and deceased, and livestock herding. When they encountered livestock while on a search mission, they ignored the animals.

6

SAR Dog Training Methods

If you have selected a dog that is eager to work and has built a bond with you, training should be relatively easy. However, methods of training SAR dogs range from kind to torturous. As early as 1848, W.N. Hutchinson, in his book *Dog Breaking: The Most Expeditious, Certain and Easy Method, Whether Great Excellence or Only Mediocrity Be Required, With Odds and Ends for Those Who Love the Dog and the Gun*, promoted positive dog training.[1]

Lieutenant-Colonel E.H. Richardson made it clear, repeatedly, when studying war dog training from the Germans, and later when he was the head of the British war dog school during the First World War, that all training should be positive.[2] Yet because of popular trainers from the Second World War and in later years the United States, as seen on television, dog training methods became harsh, even to the point of being cruel. Unfortunately, many of these methods, using pinch collars, choke collars, shock collars, and dominance methods, persist today even though modern research shows that these methods can permanently scar a dog mentally and sometimes physically. Why then do some trainers believe in them? The answer is that everything works some of the time and nothing works all the time. Some dogs can handle the harsh, punishing methods, and some cannot. During the Second World War, many of the dogs that survived the harsh methods used in the United States successfully were, in essence, pre-selected for their duties because they had already proved they would not buckle under punishing training. The dogs that could not handle these methods were washed out of the program.

Today there is no need to use these cruel, harsh methods because employing them often causes a dog to distrust humans, especially if the dog is soft. SAR dogs must love people and trust their handlers. Often it seems that people who use shock collars or, as they are called, remote trainers, are unable to successfully motivate their dogs to do the job at hand. It often takes longer to train a dog without using punishment. Just like people, dogs learn at different rates, regardless of the breed.

Two Schools of Thought for SAR Dog Training

Currently, there are two primary schools of thought that influence SAR dog training. Surprisingly, they are both based on the same concept—using a dog's prey chase or hunting instinct—and both methods work. One method has the dog stay with the found scent source and the other has the dog return to the handler, give a signal, and then lead the handler back to the scent source. Certain applications, such as HRD, water search, and disaster search, do not have the dog return to the handler. Air scenting and off-leash scent-specific work can be either, depending on the handler's preference.

Both methods involve the same beginning steps:

1. Search to find human scent, either live or deceased.
2. Work out the scent following the scent cone. One method has the dog stay with the scent source and give an alert of some kind. Another method has the dog return to you, the handler, and give an indication that he has found the scent source. Then the dog leads you back to the scent source.

3. Receive a reward. One method uses what the dog likes as a reward; it can be a toy, food, or physical and verbal praise. The other method has you toss an old sock, rope toy, or similar object to the dog. He can play with the toy until he gives it up and brings it back to you.

WHICH METHOD SHOULD YOU CHOOSE?

Both types of training work, depending upon your ability to train the dog. But more important, the head trainer or handler must be able to determine, based on the individual dog, which method will work for that dog. It is this determination that often makes or breaks a dog's ability to do SAR work successfully. For the trainers/handlers to successfully determine this, they must be experienced in dog training and know the differences between dogs and breeds.

In the end, however, it comes down to the individual dog. For example, some Labrador retrievers may have a strong hunting drive, while others may have very little. One English setter may be very "birdy," while another is not. One border collie may have high energy and want to herd everything that moves, while another is very laid back and not interested in chasing things. How you train your dog to meet his specific needs will determine how successful he will be.

7

SAR Dog Training Problems

The most important thing to keep in mind about training dogs is that *obedience is not a matter of the dog knowing what to do but is instead dependent on the dog's ability to exercise self-control to do it.* For a dog to complete an exercise, she must understand what is expected of her and then have the self-control and motivation to do it. Understanding this concept will go a long way toward helping you determine the underlying cause of a training issue.

Generalizing and Legalistic Dogs

There are basically two major types of dog, regardless of breed: those that generalize lessons and can apply what they are taught to new situations and those that are legalistic. Legalistic dogs tend to have to be taught each situation and do not readily generalize. In time, legalistic dogs will apply what they have been taught to different situations, but it takes more time. Both types of dog, if properly trained, are reliable. The main difference is the amount of time it takes to train them.

One of the big downfalls for many dogs, especially ones that tend to be legalistic, is learning dog competitive obedience exercises before SAR training. In competitive obedience, the dog is taught exactly what to do, where to do it, and when to do it. If the dog, for example, does not sit straight, she is corrected for not sitting straight and redirected into the proper position. A correction does not mean that she is punished, but her reward is withheld.

During this process, the dog learns not to think on her own, to only do what she is told. The transition to making decisions in the field can be impossible because the dog has, in a sense, been brainwashed. This is not to say that the SAR dog is permitted to disobey or not be under the control of the handler. A SAR dog must be obedient and controllable off leash in many aspects of SAR work. However, the obedience training method is different for SAR dogs than for competition dogs. For example, if the SAR dog is told to sit-stay and after a minute or so decides to lie down, but stays, this is okay. By lying down, the dog is telling her handler that she is going to stay as long as required. The main issue in the lesson is staying, not *how* the dog is staying. Giving the dog the freedom to decide how she will stay allows her to decide based on the circumstances. This concept helps the dog make decisions in the field. After all, SAR dogs must be able to exercise intelligent disobedience, just as the guide dog for a blind person must. For example, if you, the handler, try to leave an area where the subject is hidden, your dog must insist that you go to the subject and refuse to leave the area. If the blind person commands the dog to go forward and there is danger, the dog must refuse to obey.

Common Handler Mistakes

You can avoid most training problems by teaching your dog the mechanics of the search scenario before trying to search large areas or move on to more difficult problems. Most SAR dog handlers are anxious to get in the field and search, even in training. As a result, they increase the distance and difficulty of the search scenario before the dog clearly understands what is expected of her. This is one of the biggest reasons why dogs fail in one or more aspects of the search scenario. The dog should perform satisfactorily 90 per cent of the time in each step before you move on to the next step. Keep in mind that it takes repetition for a lesson to make the leap from short-term memory to long-term memory, even for a dog.

Handlers find it frustrating to watch another dog learning the steps faster than their own dogs and having to be patient as their dogs learn at their own speeds. Always remember that the combinations of handler and dog are unique. Some people have a knack for working with their dogs, while others struggle and take longer. This does not mean that the end results are necessarily different, but the fine tuning of the team's ability to work together is unique to each dog/handler team. Again, it takes an experienced dog trainer to observe the dynamics and solve the problem.

One of the biggest mistakes that handlers make is micromanaging their dogs. This undermines the dog's ability to think and reason. A SAR dog must be able to determine how to work a problem on her own. Handlers often train their dogs as if they themselves can detect the scent and know everything their dogs know. In most cases, the handlers are wrong and give their dogs the wrong message.

It takes patience for you to let your dog work out problems on her own. For example, your dog may overrun a scent trail or a scent cone, especially if she is young and/or inexperienced. If you know where the trail is, it is tempting to direct her back to the trail. This is one of the worst things you can do. If you instead let your dog lose the scent and then cast around to find it again, she will learn how to work the wind, weather, and terrain. In a real situation, you will not know where the scent is, and in a training situation you may not realize that the has scent drifted and is stronger in another location. By correcting your dog, which is what redirecting the dog does, she may think you know where the scent is and can become dependent on you for direction. If your dog thinks you know where the scent is, she may stop working. This is often why SAR dogs fail their certifications or cannot find the subject when their handlers do not know where the subject is hidden.

Another problem your dog might encounter is a different scent alongside the target scent. Redirecting her may encourage your dog to leave the target scent and follow the unknown scent. In this situation, you would be untraining your dog and most likely confusing her as to what the initial "find" command means. Never forget that training is the act of teaching the dog what the rules are and what she is to do. Mishandling a dog in training can confuse a dog so much that she cannot learn what is expected of her.

One of the most common general mistakes that handlers make is to talk to their dogs too much. This can cause dogs to become distracted, misunderstand their handlers, become confused, and stop working. The only time you should talk to your dog during a search is to tell her what to do and then praise her for doing it. This is critical for dogs that are in training and are not seasoned search dogs. The seasoned search dog can be taught a rest command and then restart when the search is resumed.

KEEPING YOUR TRAINING LOG AND SEARCH RECORDS SPOTLESS

One of the mistakes SAR dog handlers often make is to keep spotty records (or none) of their dogs' training. A meticulously kept training log not only helps you keep track of how your dog is working and what needs to be improved but is invaluable if you are asked to testify in court—and you may need to do this. A thorough log includes:

1. Details for each session: the goal of the lesson, how it was set up, how your dog worked, and what needs to be improved.

2. Details on how to improve training problems, including the steps necessary to fix the problems.

3. All physical conditions: wind, temperature, terrain, humidity, and so on.

4. How scent articles were handled and preserved from contamination by other scents.

5. Description of how your dog can correctly find or identify people or objects in blind and double-blind training conditions to verify that your dog is identifying the correct scent.
6. All failures. A training log that only boasts successes will not be taken seriously.

The court may require you to provide your search report for the mission in question. A vague search report hinders your testimony; it must have all the details about how you and your dog worked your sector. The report should include everything that might have affected the search: wind, weather, terrain, results, lack of results, and so on. Because you may have more than one assignment (or area to search) it is important to treat each assignment as a separate report. If you are assigned to search over different days and times, the conditions of the areas searched will each be unique.

If the search involved evidence, you should have properly preserved the scent associated with the evidence. For example, handling evidence with latex gloves is not proper procedure since your scent can pass through the gloves or be present on the outside of the gloves. Always use sterilized metal tongs, and note that you have done so in the report. And when you store the scented object, remember: glass, metal, and ceramic containers preserve scent the best. If the object must be stored for a while, refrigerate it at a low temperature. Include details on storage in your report, too.

The report is always a valuable tool, especially if you are called in to testify sometime after the search happened. Keep all search reports on file. Consider keeping a hard copy, just in case your e-file is lost or corrupted.

In your testimony, you may be asked to divulge confidential information about the search. Discuss this with your lawyer prior to testifying—he or she will handle confidential information. Do not, however, record any confidential information in your training log or your search reports, since these documents may be subpoenaed and made available to both parties in a court case. Instead, keep a separate file that details confidential information for your own records, so that you can correctly recall that information if called upon to do so.

Before you testify, make sure you discuss your role in the proceedings with your lawyer ahead of time. Being well-prepared is the key. Detailed search reports and training logs are essential even if you are never called to testify. They help you recall important information about your dog's training and performance that can help the two of you be the best team you can be.

Common Training Problems

Outlined below are suggestions about how to solve common training problems, but they may not work with every dog. Some dogs cannot unlearn the mistakes their handlers have made. It is impossible to tell a dog that you made a mistake and to forget what you have been doing. The dog never forgets, and in some circumstances, she may resort to what she was first taught. Therefore, it is very important to do it right the first time.

THE DOG WILL NOT GO TO THE VICTIM WHEN FOUND

This is usually a problem for air-scenting dogs but can also be a problem with scent-specific work. You begin by giving the search command and your dog does a great job of finding the hidden person, but after returning to you and giving the signal that she has found the subject, your dog will not lead you back to the hidden person.

In some cases, with this problem, the dog will stop so far away from the hidden person that the handler cannot tell where the person is located. The dog will often look at the handler as if she expects her handler to know where the person is hidden.

This is a problem because your dog should go right in to the hidden person so that you know exactly where the person is. In situations where the real missing person may be unconscious and lying in dense brush, especially a small child, you may walk by or not be able to find the hidden person if your dog does not take you right to the person. If the situation is such that it is physically impossible for the dog to get right next to the subject, the dog should point to the exact location where the subject is located.

If this is happening to you, it is usually a case of miscommunication between you and your dog that was established in the early stages of training. Likely, when you realized that your dog had found the person, instead of waiting for her to finish the scenario, you simply proceeded, often leading your dog to the hidden person. The dog learned that *looking* in the general direction of where the person is hidden is okay. Often your body language told your dog that you knew where the person was hiding. The dog knew you knew. This often happens when the handler knows at the start of the training exercise where the person is hiding.

To correct this problem, go back to the initial short runaways and have the hidden person lure your dog in. Your dog must be in a highly excited state as she is at the very start of a runaway so that she will go right in to the hidden person. The hidden person will give the dog her reward until she consistently goes in to the hidden person. Some trainers do not want the dog to receive her reward from the hidden person or subject. Their reasoning is that the dog may want to stay with the hidden person instead of returning to the handler since the hidden person has the reward.

Once the dog is consistently going in to the hidden person, she can receive her reward from you, but only after she has led you to stand next to the hidden person. Depending on the dog, the reward may have to come from either the hidden person or the handler. This is a judgment call by the dog trainer. All dogs are different and no one method works with all. Eventually, only you, the handler, should give the reward so that your dog does not stay by the hidden person waiting for her reward.

This problem can be avoided when search training is first started (from the very first lesson) and the dog only gets her reward from the handler when the handler is right next to the hidden person. This way, the dog is taught to go close to the hidden person to get her reward. Some handlers do not want their dogs to touch the hidden person, and that is okay if the dog is close enough so that the handler can see the hidden person in all scenarios.

Larry Bulanda and border collie Ness. If the dog cannot get right next to the subject, he should get as close as possible and give a clear indication as to where the subject is located.

THE DOG WILL NOT RETURN TO THE HANDLER AFTER FINDING THE HIDDEN PERSON

In this scenario, your dog will do a great find and then not return to you, but will stay with the hidden person.

This situation typically occurs because you have let the hidden person reward the dog for too long in training. Per the previous problem, who gave the reward and for how many repetitions was a judgment call made by the trainer when your dog was first learning the exercise. The trainer's choice of method can be influenced by the type of reward your dog gets. A dog that is highly motivated by food may wait with the hidden person, expecting food. For a highly food-motivated dog, food should not be the reward. This type of dog works best with a toy reward that is tossed to the dog by the handler when she completes the exercise. Handlers often think that using food for highly food-motivated dogs will increase their drive to find the hidden person, but their drive will not be to find the person but to get the food, which will affect their performance. Dogs that are ball crazy can act the same way toward a ball or another high-value toy.

If you have this problem, you know that your dog does not have a high drive to find the hidden person or lead you in to the hidden person. Instead, her focus is on the reward. There are a few ways to correct this type of problem.

One way is to eliminate the toy/food reward totally and build the dog's drive to please you, her handler. This requires a dog that already has a strong bond with you.

Start with the basic runaway as you would with a new dog. When your dog finds the hidden person, you should reward her with petting and praise. When the dog is enthusiastic about finding the hidden person, do not run in to the hidden person when she makes a find, but hang back a few yards, still within sight of the hidden person. The hidden person should not reward your dog. Give the dog time to assess the situation and then go to you for praise. At this point, you will let her lead you to the hidden person, and then praise her only when you are right next to the hidden person. If your dog does not return to you, move closer to the hidden person until she returns to you.

When your dog performs to standard at least 80 per cent of the time, you can stay farther away from the hidden person until you trust that your dog will return and lead you in.

Another way to correct this problem is to substitute a lower-value toy as a reward. A towel that the dog likes to play tug with or a ball (or another object if the dog is ball crazy) in a sock or sock-like piece of cloth all work very well. When your dog finds the hidden person, toss the cloth-covered object to her at the end of the exercise. She should be allowed to play with the sock until she willingly gives it back to you. As she learns the scenario, you can move farther away from the hidden person until she does a reliable find and refind 80 per cent of the time.

THE DOG WILL DO A GREAT FIND AND THEN ABANDON THE PROBLEM, OFTEN GOING OFF ON HER OWN

This is often a problem with the dog's drive to find people. After the excitement of the runaway, the dog becomes bored. Some dogs do not have the drive to keep going and are often distracted by other things. These dogs will not solve a long problem.

In other cases, the dog was inadvertently trained that the problem is over when she finds the missing person. In yet other cases, the reward for finishing the problem is not enough for the dog. In a few cases, the dog has not bonded with her handler enough to include the handler in the "hunt."

The scenario should be that initial runaways are highly exciting. The dog can be given the reward from the hidden person for a few sessions in the very beginning of the training if she is reluctant to go in to a hidden person, but after that, the reward must come from you, the handler. This way your dog will want to come back to you to get her reward. Once your dog understands the find game, it is important that you do not run in to the missing person immediately. As your dog progresses with the exercise, you should stay farther and farther behind, forcing her to come to you to look for her reward. Very early in the training, withhold the reward from your dog until you are next to the missing person. This way, she learns that she must bring you to the missing person to get her reward.

If your dog is motivated, she will follow the steps to complete the search, alert, and refind steps. The head trainer should watch the exercise to see which step is the one causing your dog to fail to complete the exercise; then you should all work on that part of the problem until she gets it or is washed from the program.

An example of a dog that is focused and doing his job. When the dog returns to the handler to give the signal that he has found the subject, there should be no mistake as to the signal. Rio alerting to Kay McDonald at a Deb Palman Seminar. (Photo by Paul J. Morris)

THE DOG WILL ONLY GO IN TO THE HIDDEN PERSON IF THE HANDLER KNOWS WHERE THE PERSON IS HIDDEN

This problem is also usually created in the early stages of training. Your dog will locate the hidden person but will not take you in to the hidden person. It is obvious that your dog knows where the person is by her body language, but she will not lead you to the subject. This can happen with both air-scenting dogs and scent-specific dogs, as well as dogs in other disciplines. In this case, the dog has yet to go near the hidden person. The problem is similar to but not quite the same as when the dog finds the hidden person, comes back to the handler, gives the signal, and then does not take the handler all the way back to the hidden person.

This situation can happen with first-time handlers that are very excited that their dogs have found someone, and they want to encourage the dogs to "show me." What causes the miscommunication here is that you have made it obvious to your dog that you know where the person is hidden before your dog tells you, or if your dog does a refind, before your dog leads you to the person. Often you will become excited and command, "Show me, show me," as you point to where the person is hidden and start to move in that direction. If you watch your dog, you will see that in many cases as you are saying, "Show me"—and in some cases, you are also animated and saying, "Good girl"—your dog is watching you and not focusing on the hidden person. Your dog sees that you know where the person is hidden, and she hears that she is a "good girl" while she is looking at you, her handler. Therefore, she is being praised for looking at you and not going to the hidden person. Often the next thing you do is point in the direction of the hidden person and then lead the way there. The dog thinks, "My job is done."

Research has shown that dogs do imitate the behavior of humans, so the dog will stand near the handler and point, but not go in.[1]

Another reason why your dog can misunderstand is that she thinks the exercise is finished because you know where the person is hidden.

If this has happened for several training sessions (typically a dog will learn after three experiences since that is about what it takes for memory to go from short- to long-term for a dog), it will be more difficult to correct.

To communicate the right message to your dog, it is best to go back to the beginning with runaways. The runaways can be longer, but the goal is to have your dog's excitement level very high. If possible, do not know where the volunteer has hidden. Obviously, you will have a general idea, but try not to know the specific place. Set up the runaway at a distance far enough that your dog has time to get to the hidden person before you.

If your dog is being trained to do a refind, now is the time to work on that. You will not go to the hidden person until she does her refind and leads you back to the subject. What is critical at this point is that you change your reaction to the refind. Issue a low key, "Show me." If your dog understands that command, hang back and let her lead the way. She may initially become confused and seem unsure as to what to do. In some cases, if the dog's excitement level is high, the handler can turn away or wait for the dog to sort things out, and out of frustration, try to get the handler to the hidden person. When you are shoulder to shoulder with the hidden person, give your dog her reward. In some cases, the reward may have to be intensified to keep your dog's drive high.

The main point with this problem is that you, the handler, must change your body language to convince your dog that you do not know where the person is hiding.

There is another problem related to this one. In this case the dog will do a find, refind, and take the handler in to the hidden person *only if the handler is facing the direction where the person is hidden.* In this case the dog has read a subtler form of the handler's body language and takes the position of the body or the direction of the gaze as a signal to finish the exercise.[2]

It is a good idea to have someone who is experienced in training dogs, even a non-SAR person who is a dog trainer or behavior consultant, watch the interaction between you and your dog to see exactly what form of communication is taking place so that you can change what you are doing.

Retraining your dog as explained in this section and avoiding the signals she reads is the best way to fix this issue. Your dog must learn that you never have a clue where the person is hidden until you are standing next to the person and indicate to your dog that the exercise is finished.

THE DOG WILL NOT GIVE A RELIABLE ALERT

The alert is the signal your dog should give you after she has found the hidden person and before doing the refind. The dog should find, return to you and give the active alert (which is usually some

SAR DOG TRAINING PROBLEMS

Larry Bulanda and Ness air scenting. It is important that the handler follows the dog and does not interfere with the dog working. In this photo, Ness is leading Larry to the subject.

sort of bark, unique behavior, body bang, etc.), then lead you to the hidden person. The alerts given for other exercises—identifying the scent source in scent-specific work such as trailing/tracking, HRD, water body recovery, and so on—are passive (lying down or sitting near the scent source). If she does not reliably display the alert she has been trained to perform, you have a problem.

It cannot be stressed enough that you *do not* try to teach your dog what the alert is during search training. Learning is different than applying what has been learned.

There are two ways to handle the alert. The first is to teach your dog what you want the alert to be. This works with some dogs and not as well with others. Examples of taught alerts are a bark, holding a bringsel, or physical contact. Some people claim that they read their dog's body language. This is not a reliable means to determine if your dog has found a missing person. It is important to be able to read your dog, but do not rely on body language as the only, clear, unmistakable signal that she has found the missing person.

Larry Bulanda and border collie Jib. It is important for the handler to follow the dog and not clue the dog as to where the subject is hidden.

An example of the focus a dog must have in SAR work. Kay McDonald's Poppy gives an alert on HRD. (Photo by Paula Wickman)

Another way to determine the alert is by letting your dog do what comes naturally for her when she tries to tell you she has found the missing person. An example of this is the dog hitting you with her feet or body in a specific way, as hearing dogs alert their deaf companions when the phone rings or the doorbell chimes. Rewarding this behavior will teach your dog to do it reliably. Some dogs will grab an item of your clothing to signal an alert. This is okay if the item is always available for the dog to grab. Some dogs have been known to grab the handler's hand or arm to try to lead them to their find.

Keep in mind that different breeds will instinctively alert in certain ways, just because it feels right to them. For example, boxers may want to hit you with their feet while retrievers will want to put something in their mouth.

Whatever the alert is, you must be able to identify it during the day, night, and in noisy and other distracting situations. In the case of disaster, HRD, water body location, and so on, the alert should be passive, wherein the dog does not return to the handler. No matter what the situation is, your dog must always be able to give the alert.

The key reason why dogs fail to give a reliable alert is because they think you already know they have found what you are looking for. Why would your dog think this? The answer lies in some of the latest research about what dogs understand. As mentioned earlier in this book, dogs can follow where you point. Most people think this means pointing your finger, but we know that dogs can follow your gaze, and read your facial expressions and emotions.[3] Some dogs pay more attention to the handler's reactions than others do. If you get very vocal and animated as soon as your dog finds the subject, you may draw attention to yourself. Dogs that enjoy getting this reaction from their handlers may think that this is enough and not feel they must give the alert. Yes, you do want to praise your dog when she does things right, but the timing is critical. Animation and praise should only come after your dog has completed the exercise.

The key to getting your dog to tell you everything is to make her think that you cannot see, hear, detect odors, or otherwise know what she knows. This is why it is so important that you transition as quickly as possible to training sessions where you really do not know where the missing person is hiding. Then you cannot inadvertently indicate to your dog that you know she found the missing person or even indicate where the person is hiding before the dog finds him or her.

It is always best to avoid the problem or prevent the problem rather than to cure it. In early training, never look in the direction where the volunteer is hiding. Also, avoid slowing down, hesitating, or otherwise giving any body language signal when you are near the volunteer.

If your dog already thinks you know where the volunteer is hidden, then you should have someone watch your dog solve a few problems over a few training sessions and try to see what signal you are giving her. Once that is established, you can make sure not to give that signal anymore. If what your dog sees is not obvious to you, change direction as if you are going to grid in another area. If her drive is strong, your dog will become frustrated and try to get you to go toward the hidden volunteer. As soon as she does this, acknowledge her signal and let her lead you in to the volunteer.

THE DOG CHASES CRITTERS OR GAME

There are a few reasons why a dog will divert from SAR work to chase game. One is that the dog's hunting/prey chase instinct is strong and she cannot resist chasing game. Two, the dog is not motivated enough to find people. Or three, the dog has been encouraged to chase game, either as a puppy or by a previous owner or someone in the family unbeknownst to the handler.

Keep in mind that not every dog is "people minded," and some would rather do something else. Some dogs are only interested in finding their owners and no one else. These dogs can be diverted easily by other animals.

The best way to solve this problem is prevention. However, the following can be used on any dog. Keep in mind that a dog with experience chasing game will be much more difficult if not impossible to train to ignore game. This will depend on how long the dog has been chasing game and how biddable the dog is.

When your dog is young, still a puppy or as soon as you have adopted her and bonded after a few weeks, she must be taught to "leave it." The actual words you use do not matter as much as the concept.

When you say, "leave it," you communicate to your dog that she will never get the object that she is being told to leave. It means get away as fast as you can—danger. The command "don't touch," on the other hand, means she can look at the object and eventually may be told to "take it."

Place a low-value item such as a glove or hat in an area where you can walk your dog. Put her on a leash and walk her within sight of the object. Each time you do this exercise approach from a different angle or direction.

When the dog first notices the object, immediately reverse walking. Do not take the time to turn around, but back up away from the object as you command, "Leave it!" in a tone that communicates "danger." Move away as fast as you can. As soon as your dog stops trying to look at the object (a head harness makes this easier to do), stop and praise her. Continue to do this once or twice a day, with time between each session, until she refuses to look at the object and will turn away when she hears the command. Once your dog gets the idea, she will notice the object and then look at you and move away from the object.

The next step is to use an object your dog will find more interesting than the glove. Continue this exercise until the dog is good 90 per cent of the time.

Next, substitute the previous object for fake or real fur, such as a fur collar from an old coat. Second-hand shops are a good source for this. Place the fur outside and repeat the exercise. When the dog demonstrates self-control, you can move on to the next level of training.

With the help of another person, tie a very long string or fishing line to the fur and have your helper hide behind something, out of sight and downwind from your dog. (The wind should be blowing from the dog to the person.) On your signal, such as tapping the top of your head, have the person jerk the string to make the fur jump. Only do this once. As soon as the dog looks at the object give the "leave it" command. Repeat this exercise, increasing the distance the fur moves until the helper can pull the fur across an area and your dog will still walk away and not look or try to go to the fur. This will take several training sessions over a period of days or weeks, depending on how often you work with your dog.

At this point you are ready to try the command relative to live animals. Use whatever type of animal you can obtain or go near to train the dog. All types of animals are acceptable, since wildlife comes in all sizes. Initially, use the head harness. This way, if your dog cannot resist the animal, you will still have control of her head and be able to prevent injury to either the dog or the animal.

It is always a good idea, once the dog masters the exercise, to refresh her occasionally by using the "leave it" command around a variety of animals and objects. The "leave it" command can also be used with objects your dog may come across in the field, such as animal droppings, food, or carcasses.

THE DOG DOES WELL WITH SHORT PROBLEMS BUT FAILS TO SOLVE LONGER PROBLEMS

The first thing you must do, especially if your dog is of a breed prone to hip dysplasia, elbow problems, back issues, or arthritis, is to have your dog checked by a veterinarian to ensure there is not a medical reason why she will only do short problems. Even a young dog can suffer from medical issues.

If the dog is okay physically, often the cause of this type of problem is that you did not move ahead in the runaway stage of training but continued to do short problems. Often handlers do this because they expect their dogs to perform 100 per cent correctly before moving on to the next stage of training. No dog ever works at 100 per cent all the time. There are many variables that will cause a dog to work a bit under par. And just like humans, dogs can have a bad day.

If you continue to do short problems when your dog is ready to move on, your dog learns that "search" means short problems.

Another reason this problem can happen is because your dog is not motivated enough—her excitement level is too short-lived. One reason for a lack of motivation is that the reward is not strong enough for her to find the hidden person when it requires more work.

The best way to solve this problem is to give your dog a rest from SAR work for a few weeks. During that time, test your dog to see what reward seems to motivate her the most. What you determine is a good reward may not be what she considers a good reward.

After a rest, start her on a short runaway, but release her only when she is very excited. Give your dog a short rest and then set up another runaway, but make the distance twice as far. Still allow her to see the helper run away. Only allow your dog to find the helper when he or she is out of sight and your dog's excitement is very high. Do this as you gradually increase the distance until your helper is too far away for your dog to easily see. The goal is to make your dog use her nose and keep her interest high. Do not be afraid to stay at this training level until your dog shows excitement at the prospect of searching.

If the above method does not work for your dog, switch places with the helper and let the assistant handle the dog. This should motivate your dog to search longer distances. As soon as she shows enthusiasm at the prospect of searching, the helper can hide again.

Be sure that your dog does not get her reward until you are standing next to the hidden helper. She must understand that there is no reward unless she finds the person and you are present.

As soon as she shows enthusiasm at the prospect of searching, the problems should be made longer until she will search for the required amount of time to complete a mission.

THE DOG STOPS WORKING

In some cases, a dog that has been working well will start to fail at SAR work. One main reason is that the dog has become old. What is considered old for a dog depends on the breed of the dog and the individual dog's genetics. Most large dogs—i.e., German shepherds, golden retrievers, Labrador retrievers, and other breeds of that size—have a good working life, until they are about eight years old. After that they begin to fail. The problem is that they do not fail quickly but will age slowly, the same as humans. Each of their senses can diminish. Dogs also suffer from dementia and can act confused. Your dog is showing signs of aging or illness if she:

1. Moves slower;
2. Cannot search as long;
3. Loses the scent more often, especially in situations where she normally excels;
4. Shows aggression or avoidance toward other animals or people;
5. Does not obey at the same level she used to; or
6. Does not respond to audio commands or visual commands the same as she used to.

Keep in mind that older dogs (and sometimes younger dogs) suffer from illnesses that have gone undetected because there are no tests for them, such as cancer of the spleen and other forms of cancer that must be detected using imaging methods to be caught early.

Sometimes a dog will fail because the handler has lost faith in the dog's ability to search. This is most likely to happen with an inexperienced SAR dog handler who has not learned to trust the dog. As we have seen throughout this book, dogs are very good at reading their handlers' feelings and body language. Dogs that are especially sensitive to their handlers may become discouraged by their handlers' attitude and/or body language. In this case, for the team's sake, a good trainer should work with the handler and set up problems where the dog cannot fail so that the handler can learn to read the dog and regain faith in her. The training should also include situations where there is no subject to be found. It is just as important to trust the dog when there is nothing to be found as it is to trust the dog when she finds the object of the search. Teaching the dog an "all clear" signal helps both dog and handler when there is nothing to be found.

In real searches, clearing a sector usually means that the missing person or object is not in the sector. This happens more often than being the lucky person who is assigned to the sector where the missing person is found. It is also important that you, the SAR dog handler, understand that even the best dog in the prime of condition can have an off day, or due to climatic situations cannot locate the scent. This does not mean your dog has lost the ability to search.

THE DOG SEEMS TO LOSE THE SCENT

This problem is especially noticeable in scent-specific dogs. Your dog may have drive, stamina, and enthusiasm but loses the scent after following it for a short distance.

This is a very complicated problem because you can never be sure that the scent is there for your dog to follow. In areas where the weather changes quickly, temperature can affect the scent. If a helper is hiding after having traveled a distance to go into the hiding place, and it is cool or cold out, the scent is more readily available for your dog to detect. This is because a person who has exercised gives off more heat and thus scent. On the other hand, if the person is hidden under a waterproof covering and it is warm out, the scent is more difficult for your dog to detect. Even if the helper is not under a waterproof covering, warm objects in warm weather are more difficult for dogs to find. Cold objects in a cold environment are difficult to find, as well.

Chemicals can temporarily block scent for a dog. This can occur in the field. For example, mountain laurel and related plants can nullify human scent. Dogs cannot find scent in dense patches of mountain laurel because of a chemical that the plants give off. You should not try to train an inexperienced dog in areas with mountain laurel.

If it is necessary to search an area where the scent may be destroyed, such as a stand of mountain laurel, you can send your dog into the "caves" that often exist at the base of the plant in hope that she will stumble upon the missing person. In this type of situation, a closely spaced grid team should work behind you and your dog. You must realize that the probability of detection (POD) will be low in this scenario. You also must let your dog work on her own as much as possible, knowing that she will not find scent either in the path where the subject walked or be able to pick up a scent cone. What we do not know is how quickly the target scent is destroyed by these types of plants.

Other chemicals can temporarily block your dog's nose so she cannot detect a weaker scent. Typically, this only lasts for a few minutes. Dogs, just like people, can suffer from colds, viruses,

MOUNTAIN LAUREL

Mountain laurel and its cousins give off a gas that can flood a dog's nose and kill any scent under and around it. Also, the foliage is so dense that if a person hid under the canopy of the bush, scent cannot survive. The leaves are broad, thick, and waxy. The scent in the immediate area around the bush is also destroyed. Mountain laurel is a member of the heath family or *Ericaceae*. This family of plants includes huckleberries, blueberries, azaleas, cranberries, and rhododendrons. Mountain laurel is a shrub but can grow up to 12 meters (40 feet) high in southern states. Typically, they do not grow higher than 3 meters (10 feet). They are most common in hilly, rocky locations. Sheep laurel and bog laurel, related to mountain laurel, grow in the northern states and in Canada. There are over 75 domestic varieties of mountain laurel.

---

and allergies that can make it difficult or impossible for them to detect scent.

Another reason why some dogs cannot detect scent is because of the structure of their nose. Short-nosed breeds with "pushed in" faces such as pugs and Boston terriers do not have the scenting ability of the long-nosed breeds. Also, albino dogs are not as capable of detecting odors as non-albino dogs.[4] However, small dogs such as Jack Russell terriers, Havanese, papillon, and other small breeds, have the same ability to detect scent as large dogs.

If a dog has been following a scent for a while, she may rest her nose by moving it away from the scent and then go back to it. When your dog does this, do not think that she has lost the scent or has stopped working. It is important to always give your dog time to work out the problem without interfering.

Another reason why a dog may seem to be losing the scent is because of handler error. This usually occurs because the handler does not trust the dog.

As is already noted, one of the biggest mistakes you can make is to re-command your dog to search for or follow a scent. When you do this, you may be commanding her to follow a different scent than the one you initially told your dog to follow. This can happen if your dog stops or slows down to work out a scent picture because other scents have mingled with the scent she is following and as she tests a different scent, you re-commanded her to follow the scent. You may think your dog knows which scent you are talking about, but she may start to follow another scent because at the time of the command she was checking out a new scent. If the new scent leads to a human who is not the subject being followed, you may lose faith in your dog, thinking she failed, when in fact she did exactly as you commanded.

In all disciplines of search work, it is best not to talk to your dog while she is working. Talking only distracts her and can cause her to become confused. A good working dog will continue to work without being prodded by her handler. However, taking a rest is a different issue. It is okay to stop to let a dog rest when the dog shows fatigue. However, the commands to stop and start should be different than the command to follow a specific scent. With an air-scenting dog it is okay to re-command the dog to find, but with the scent-specific dog and in some cases with the air-scenting dog, it is better to have a "let's get back to work" command if there is a short rest. Giving the air-scenting dog the command to find again is acceptable since the dog is looking for any human scent, not a particular one. For example, the team may stop to rest for the night and resume the search in the morning or, due to the weather, have to stop searching for a few hours. If the scent-specific dog is given a long rest or interruption in the search, the handler may want to re-scent the dog when they resume the search. To the dog, it will seem like a totally new problem. Some handlers feel safer if they have the scent article with them to let the dog sniff the article before starting to search again.

Keep in mind that we do not know exactly what the scent picture looks like (or smells like) to our dogs. A scent trail for your dog can be made of many different scents. It can consist of the clothing that the subject is wearing, including the material that the clothing is made of, shoes and outer garments, the family scent, any perfumed products, as well as soil types. Soil from a backyard garden will have different components and minerals than soil from a farmer's field, woodland, forest, and areas around water. There is always the scent of animals that live in the area, both tame and wild. All these scents will mingle with the target scent your dog is looking for.

Another reason why a dog that is working on a tracking harness may stop working is if you jerk on the leash while she is working. This can be a major problem if you have used leash jerks to correct your dog. A dog should be left alone to work on her own. The tension that the dog puts on the leash is not the same as a leash jerk. Almost all scent-specific dogs that work in tracking harness will pull on the leash, but the dogs know the difference between their pulling and your leash jerking.

Keep in mind that dogs work differently. Some dogs work quickly; others work slowly. One is not better than the other. If you try to force your dog to work the way you want instead of allowing her to work in a way that is natural to her, she will become frustrated and the work will become unpleasant for her. If this continues long enough, she will stop working, which has nothing to do with her ability to follow the scent. However, handlers in this situation will often misread what is happening and think their dogs have lost the scent.

Although this book is not a "how to train the dog" book, it is important to mention that in scent-specific work, training methods can cause dogs to dislike the work, which results in them not wanting to work or not working as well as they could. If your dog does not like the work, she may quit in the middle of a scent trail. Force training the dog will not make the dog a happy scent dog. A dog that does not like to work may display fatigue, nervousness, and lack of drive, or some dogs may pretend to follow a scent but not actually follow the scent. A good SAR dog should and must love to do SAR work.

The training method used for the scent-specific dog can also affect your dog's ability to think on her own. Typically, forced training and using food as the lure to teach a dog to follow a track (food in the footprints) does not teach your dog to think on her own, and when faced with a real problem where she must decide where to go, she lacks the ability to strike out on her own.

If a dog that has been successful in following or finding scent in any SAR discipline starts to have difficulty, and the training methods have been positive, then you must consider your dog's health. All SAR work requires that the dog's senses be up to par. A veterinary examination is the first step. Eyes, ears, nose, and overall physical health must be good for a dog to work well. As your dog ages, some of her physical and mental abilities may diminish. The problem is that in most cases age takes its toll gradually and you may think that your dog is only having a bad day. If the bad days happen more and more frequently, it could be a sign of aging. Blood work such as a geriatric profile may be a good course of action for the older dog. It is also important to consider things like arthritis, a pulled muscle, and so on.

If your dog is in good health, has had positive training, and still seems to stop working or seems to lose the scent, it may be a good idea to give the dog a break from training/working. Dogs may suffer from mental fatigue just as humans do. Most SAR dog handlers try to work their dogs at least once a week and sometimes more often. Give your dog a break for two to four weeks. Only do relaxing thing with her. When you start training again, keep the problems very short to increase her drive, and watch to see if she shows any signs of physical problems. Have someone who is not familiar with your dog watch her for anything unusual. Slight limps may go unnoticed by you but will stand out to someone who knows dogs but is not used to seeing your dog's gait. If all seems okay, work on longer problems with each training session until you work up to the dog's normal capacity. Hopefully this will get your dog back on track.

Conclusion: Preventing Problems Before They Start

Overall, prevention is the best way to troubleshoot. Ensure you choose the right dog for the job, pick the best training methods for the dog, keep your dog healthy, and ensure your own training and experience is up to the task.

Choose the Right Dog
This means having the right dog for the job. The dog must be physically able to do the tasks that you want to train him to do; he must be willing to obey but able to work independently. It is essential that the dog has the drive to find, be willing to share his find with the handler, be tough enough and/or brave enough to work in adverse conditions, be intelligent, not be aggressive to humans or other animals, not have a prey drive that is directed to chasing other animals, and be able to exhibit enough self-control to do what is asked of him. Remember, obedience is not a matter of knowing what to do but the ability to exercise self-control to do what you want rather then what your dog wants.

Use Positive, Professional Training Methods

Success depends upon using positive training methods and avoiding force methods that use pinch, prong, electric, and otherwise painful collars. There are other force methods for training, such as toe pinch and groin pinch methods, that are also not conducive to your dog's mental well-being and desire to work.

Using a professional dog trainer to help you teach your dog is also a wise choice. A good dog trainer does not have to understand SAR work to be able to teach your dog the objectives of the lesson, although it helps.

Realizing that not all methods work the same for all dogs is important. That does not mean that you should use negative methods, but rather that you must "tweak" the proper/positive method to teach some dogs. The little things count in dog training.

Having a good assistant who can watch you for hidden body clues to avoid signaling your dog is essential. This is also where a good, qualified dog trainer can help.

It is also essential that you understand how to teach your dog the lessons and do not try to teach him too many things at once. Each lesson should have one main goal. As your dog learns, each lesson should build on the last lesson. It is important not to move ahead in training until your dog fully understands and has mastered each level.

A happy SAR dog is one that has not been overworked to the point where SAR work is no longer fun. In areas where there are a lot of searches, this may mean that your dog is not used in every one of them. Your dog needs a break between searches. In some cases, a day is enough, but other dogs may require a few days between searches. This depends on the dog and his handler. Handler fatigue can hinder the dog's ability to work as well.

Ensure Your Dog's Physical and Mental Fitness

Make sure your dog is physically and mentally fit, especially as he ages. Dogs can suffer from diseases such as cancer that will not show up in normal blood work and may show little or no symptoms until the very end.

A good diet is important for overall success. Only a high-quality dog food is good for a working dog. Nothing that can be purchased at a discount store or super market is high quality. Take a look at the Dog Food Advisor (https://www.dogfoodadvisor.com/dog-food-reviews/brand/) to ensure the food you are feeding

---

QUALITY DOG FOOD

The search for a good-quality dog food can be a confusing one. Reading the labels does not give you the whole picture. While it is true that the ingredients must be listed according to their percentage, ingredient lists are often misleading. For example, the first ingredient may be beef at 15 per cent of the total ingredients, and all the next ingredients are in descending order, being less than 15 per cent. However, all the lesser ingredients in combination equal 85 per cent of the food. So, they are critical to the health of the dog.

The other issue with food is where the fat comes from. Many food companies use leftover restaurant fat, which has been sitting in 55-gallon drums in all kinds of weather and has become rancid. By using an accepted (not necessarily good) processing method, they can add it to dog food.[1]

The other issue with dog food is the quality of the ingredients. If the company does not use human-grade meat, the animals may have been diseased, died of natural causes, or euthanized and collected later, or the parts of the animals used were not fit for human consumption due to tumors, and so on. If a dog food label only says "meat," the ingredients could include any kind of meat and other parts of animals not used for human consumption.

If the dog food is made by companies that produce other types of food for humans, they may include fillers made from the leftovers from the human food, such as the millings or cereal fines (the dust from making cereal).

The quality of the food you give your dog is critical to his health, working ability, and long life. It's worth it to do some research!

your dog is of the right quality. Remember that manufacturers can change the quality of their food over time, so it is wise to check on a yearly basis to be sure the food you are using is still good. Poor food will hinder your dog's ability to work as well as his long-term health. The author, a certified behavior consultant, has found that changing the brand/quality of dog food can help to alter unwanted behaviors and poor performance. A young dog (two years and younger) will not show the physical effects of poor quality food, but as your dog ages, he will gradually suffer. However, young dogs on poor food often behave differently, with hyperactivity being the most common behavior. Taking your dog to the training field after feeding him a poor-quality breakfast is like sending a child to school when she has had a sugar-based breakfast. The young dog will learn better and be calmer on a high-quality diet.

Look After Your Own Training

Your skill as a SAR handler is critical to the success of your dog. A good SAR dog handler is first and foremost a trained rescue person who specializes in deploying the dog as one of many tools used on a search mission. This is no different than the police officer who is trained as a member of the police force first and then specializes in the use of the police dog. Or the solider who is trained as a military person who then becomes a canine handler.

This means you must be dedicated to SAR, earn your unit's required certifications, and seek the best help when training your dog. Your dog also must earn his certifications to be qualified to participate in search missions.

If you want to become a SAR dog handler, you must realize that you can spend your whole career in a unit and never have a find. This does not reflect negatively on you or your dog. Typically, only one person finds the missing subject out of all the team members. However, no find can be accomplished without the help of all the team members.

As a unit and/or an individual SAR member, it is always helpful to be connected to other SAR personnel. A good way to do this is to join an umbrella organization. The National Search Dog Alliance (http://www.n-sda.org/) is an excellent group to be a member of. There are many opportunities to learn and share through this organization.

A Rewarding Career in SAR

Even though volunteer SAR handlers must pay for their own equipment, the cost of the dog and his care, and give up a lot of personal time, they find the experience very rewarding. It is a way to give back to the community, to help people and provide educational opportunities to organizations and schools. Programs for children explaining how to avoid getting lost and how to stay safe if they do get lost have saved many lives. There is a special joy and bond that you develop with your dog that is unlike any other. It is impossible to put into words. SAR can take over a person's life in a good way. The author and her husband have spent collectively over 50 years in the field. We had to give up vacations, use sick leave from jobs, and spend almost every weekend and many hours during the week to maintain our SAR unit and train our volunteer members. The time we spent in SAR work was some of the best years of our life. Ironically, when we did get to go on a vacation, the dogs went with us as well as our basic equipment, and almost every time we wound up on a search in whatever area we were vacationing.

My husband has retired from SAR due to his full-time job. I, on the other hand, am a founding member of the National Search Dog Alliance (NSDA) and still mentor handlers and try to help by writing books and a column in the NSDA newsletter, which you can access at http://www.n-sda.org/news-newsletter.php.

Getting involved in your local K9 SAR unit offers a wealth of education and experience. And you do not have to own a dog to take part. Every unit has the same needs as any volunteer organization or business. Skilled professionals can help in all capacities and volunteer as little or as much as they can. This is also true for umbrella organizations such as NSDA. Volunteering with SAR organizations will enrich your life.

Notes

Finding a Good SAR Dog

1. University of Helsinki, "How Dogs See Your Emotions: Dogs View Facial Expressions Differently," *ScienceDaily* (January 19, 2016), www.sciencedaily.com/releases/2016/01/160119074313.htm.
2. University of Florida, "DNA Studies Reveal that Shelter Workers Often Mislabel Dogs as 'Pit Bulls,'" *ScienceDaily* (February 17, 2016), www.sciencedaily.com/releases/2016/02/160217140622.htm.
3. Carmen L. Battaglia, "Early Neurological Stimulation," Breeding Better Dogs, www.breedingbetterdogs.com/article/early-neurological-stimulation. See also http://www.kitsapcanine.com/articles/SuperDog.pdf.
4. Dan G. O'Neill, Noel R. Coulson, David B. Church, Dave C. Brodbelt, "Demography and Disorders of German Shepherd Dogs Under Primary Veterinary Care in the UK," *Canine Genetics and Epidemiology*, 4 no. 1 (2017), DOI: 10.1186/s40575-017-0046-4, www.sciencedaily.com/releases/2017/07/170727221255.htm.
5. Battaglia, "Early Neurological Stimulation."

Why Dogs Have Training Problems

1. University of Chicago Medical Center, "Genomes of Modern Dogs and Wolves Provide New Insights on Domestication," *ScienceDaily* (January 16, 2014), www.sciencedaily.com/releases/2014/01/140116190137.htm.
2. Ryan Grenoble, "Dogs Can Be Optimistic or Pessimistic Just Like People, Study Shows," *The Huffington Post* (September 23, 2014), http://www.huffingtonpost.ca/entry/dogs-optimists-pessimists_n_5863670. The "Canine Sense and Sensibility" study was published in the September 17, 2015, issue of the journal *PLOS ONE*.
3. Cell Press, "Dogs Know That Smile on Your Face," *ScienceDaily* (February 12, 2015) www.sciencedaily.com/releases/2015/02/150212131647.htm.
4. University of Veterinary Medicine, Vienna. "What Are You Looking At? Dogs Are Able to Follow Human Gaze," *ScienceDaily* (June 12, 2015), www.sciencedaily.com/releases/2015/06/150612091146.htm.

5. Public Library of Science, "Dogs Succeed while Chimps Fail at Following Finger Pointing: Chimpanzees Have Difficulty Identifying Object of Interest Based on Gestures," *ScienceDaily* (February 8, 2012), www.sciencedaily.com/releases/2012/02/120208180251.htm.

What Is Scent?

1. Le Centre National de la Recherche Scientifique, "Forensic Odorology Scientifically Validated," *ScienceDaily* (February 12, 2016), www.sciencedaily.com/releases/2016/02/160212102429.htm.
2. Northwestern McCormick School of Engineering, "Whiskers Help Animals Sense the Direction of the Wind," August 24, 2016, http://www.mccormick.northwestern.edu/news/articles/2016/08/whiskers-help-animals-sense-winds-direction.html.
3. See the Appendix for more information about scent and the different factors affecting your dog's ability to follow it.

SAR Dog Training Methods

1. Lieut.-Col. E.H. Richardson and Mrs. Richardson, *Fifty Years with Dogs* (London: Hutchinson & Co., 1950).
2. Ibid. See also Major E.H. Richardson, *War, Police and Watch Dogs* (Edinburgh and London: William Blackwood and Sons, 1910); Lieut.-Col E.H. Richardson, *Watch-Dogs: Their Training and Management* (London: Hutchinson & Co. Paternoster Row, 1924); and Lieut.-Col. E.H Richardson, *Forty Years with Dogs* (Philadelphia" David McKay Company, 1930).

SAR Dog Training Problems

1. University of Helsinki, "How Dogs See Your Emotions."
2. University of Veterinary Medicine, "What Are You Looking At?"; Public Library of Science, "Dogs Succeed While Chimps Fail"; Emory Health Sciences, "Dogs Process Faces in Specialized Brain Area."
3. Emory Health Sciences, "Dogs Process Faces in Specialized Brain Area, Study Reveals: Face-Selective Region Has Been Identified in the Temporal Cortex of Dogs," *ScienceDaily* (August 4, 2015), www.sciencedaily.com/releases/2015/08/150804073709.htm; Natalia Albuquerque, Kun Guo, Anna Wilkinson, Carine Savalli, Emma Otta, and Daniel Mills, "Dogs Recognize Dog and Human Emotions," (January 13, 2016), DOI: 10.1098/rsbl.2015.0883, http://rsbl.royalsocietypublishing.org/content/12/1/20150883; University of Veterinary Medicine, "What Are You Looking At?"; Public Library of Science, "Dogs Succeed While Chimps Fail"; University of Helsinki, "How Dogs See Your Emotions."
4. Popat N. Patil, *Discoveries in Pharmacological Sciences* (Columbus: Ohio State University, 2012), 300.

Conclusion

1. Susan Thixton, "Pet Food Facts," *Dogs Naturally Magazine*, http://www.dogsnaturallymagazine.com/pet-food-fats/. See also "What's Really in Pet Food?" http://www.k-9kraving.com/pet-food-reality.

Appendix

Following Scent

Scent

Many factors affect how scent behaves: humidity, wind, lack of wind/breeze, air temperature, and terrain features. Knowing these conditions will help you, the handler, avoid mistakes in handling/reading your dog. By avoiding mistakes and understanding why your dog is behaving the way he is, you can avoid corrections or re-commanding him, which causes training problems.

Scent Cone

As scent leaves the source, it fans out in a scent cone. What is important to keep in mind is that the scent cone does not fan out

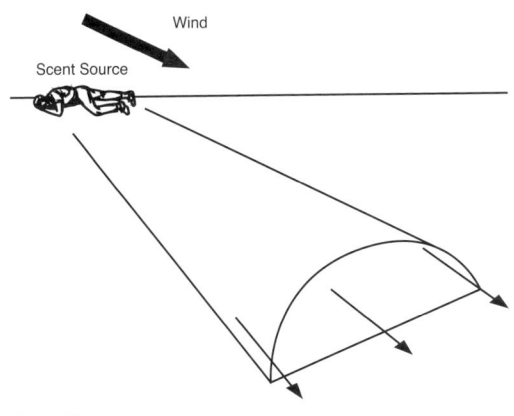

A.1 The scent cone.

in a neat manner but spreads according to the weather and air currents. It can travel in any direction and even split apart as it travels around barriers.

Scent Loops

Scent can rise until it reaches a thermocline (air level controlled by temperature changes) and then loop back to the ground. Your dog will only pick up scent pools on the ground. Some dogs will put their nose in the air where the scent rises, but they can become confused about how to follow the rising scent. As dogs gain experience searching, they learn how to work out this type of problem. New dogs may circle in the scent pool and not be sure what to do. It is best to allow them time to work it out. Once they learn that there will be multiple scent pools when pools are near each other, they will look around on the ground for the next one. Do not try to guide your dog since you will have no idea where the next scent pool is, if there is one. The scent can travel high enough that it will not come back down for quite a distance. If your dog stops working at a scent pool, sometimes it helps to let him rest and then start the problem again. Since the dog's job is to find scent, the dog is correct to identify the scent pool even if it is localized.

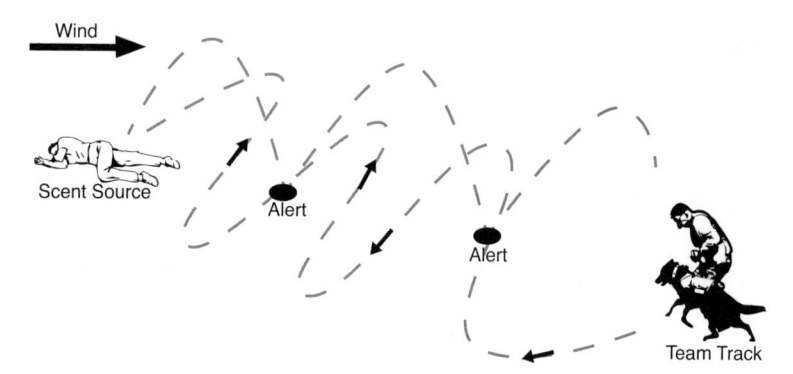

A.2 Scent loops.

Dead Zone

The size of a dead zone—a place along the scent trail where your dog loses the scent—depends on all the weather conditions as well as the terrain features. Dead zones can be caused by buildings and other humanmade obstructions as well as terrain features. It is up to you to determine whether or not your dog has encountered a dead zone and realize that in some cases the scent source may be coming down from a higher region. The scent can travel quite far under certain conditions. If you are working above a dead zone due to shifting wind conditions and continue to search at the lower level, your dog may lose the scent until he goes beyond the dead zone. However, keep in mind that you should be working your dog into the wind toward the dead zone as is illustrated in Figure A.3.

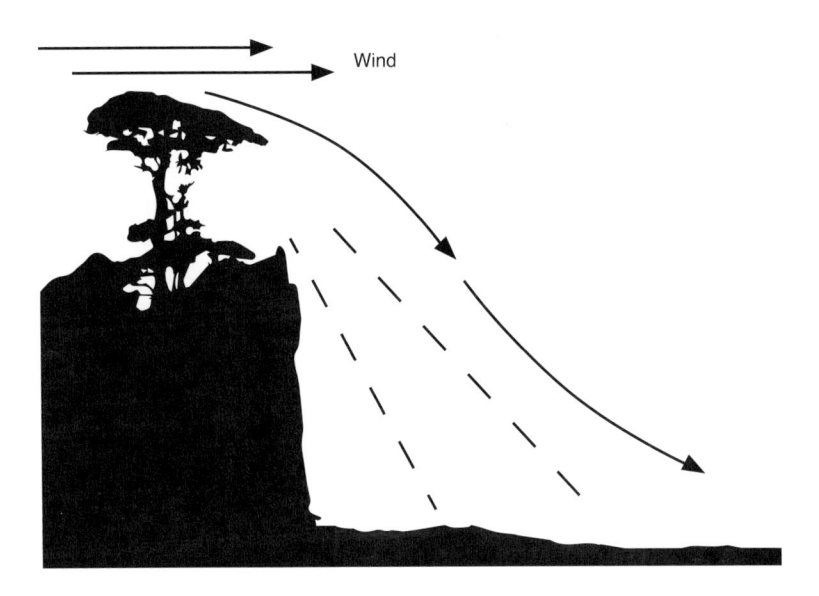

A.3 A dead zone at the bottom of a cliff.

Water Searching

To conduct a successful water search, you must determine the direction in which the water current is traveling and about how fast, as well as the wind direction. A body in the water will give off gases that will travel with the current until they reach the surface of the water, where they continue to travel with air currents. It takes special water and wind conditions for your dog to find scent directly above a missing person. Water turbulence, such as that resulting from waterfalls, boat motors, and partial dams, will also determine where the scent meets the air currents. If the scent in water meets an obstacle, such as a pier for a bridge or a dock, it can hit the obstacle and travel to the surface and then be carried by air currents.

If a body of water has a lot of organic matter on the bottom—animals that have fallen in and died, tree trunks and stumps (often found in humanmade lakes)—especially if the water has a weak current or no current, the water at the bottom may be warmer. As the warm water meets the cooler water it could form several layers or thermoclines. This can also happen in reverse, when the water is cooler on the bottom and warmer at the top. The scent can be trapped and travel along the thermocline until it reaches a break and can rise. It helps to drop rocks from a boat to break the thermocline and allow the scent to rise to the surface.

If the search is on a frozen body of water, there will be thermoclines (the coldest water is the frozen water on the surface). The scent *can* rise to the surface of the ice, and your dog *can* detect it. Ice is porous and the scent can travel through it. However, it will take longer to rise through ice. Cutting holes in the ice and dropping a few rocks to break up the thermoclines will help your dog locate the general area of the body.

FOLLOWING SCENT

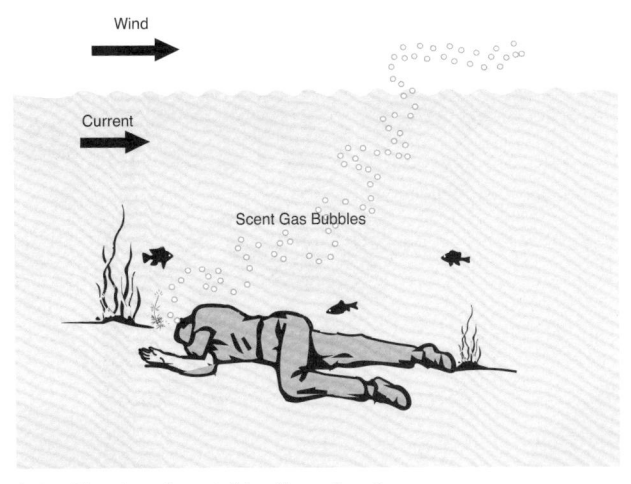

A.4 Direction of scent rising through water.

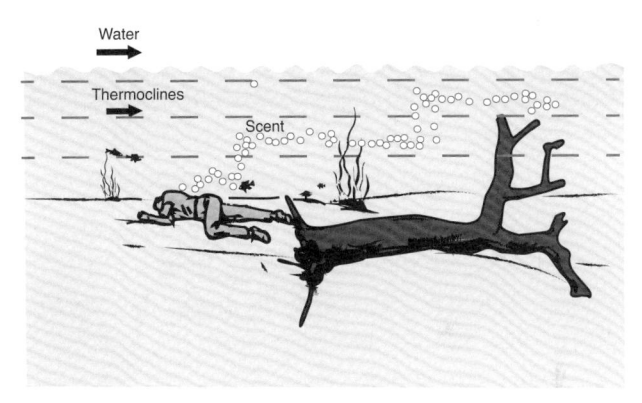

A.5 Direction of scent rising through water with thermoclines.

Fall and Rise

Depending on the weather, scent can travel along the ground and fall into a decline or rise out of a decline. The weather conditions will determine which one will happen. Typically, as the ground warms in the morning, scent tends to rise with it. In the evening, as the air cools and drops, so will the scent.

A.6 Scent rises as the ground warms.

A.7 Scent drops as the air cools in the night.

The Path of Least Resistance

Scent travels much like water, following the path of least resistance. If the search area has a fair amount of vegetation in the form of trees and brush, scent will travel through the open and less dense areas, and then if it travels into a relatively clear area, such as an open field, it will go the way the air currents take it.

When scent hits a natural or humanmade obstacle, it can scatter in several directions. It is important to remember that scent has no substance that makes it stay together. Figure A.9 shows three possible routes that a scent could take. Scent Path 1 goes up the cliff and could change direction slightly and follow the ground

A.8 Scent follows the path of least resistance.

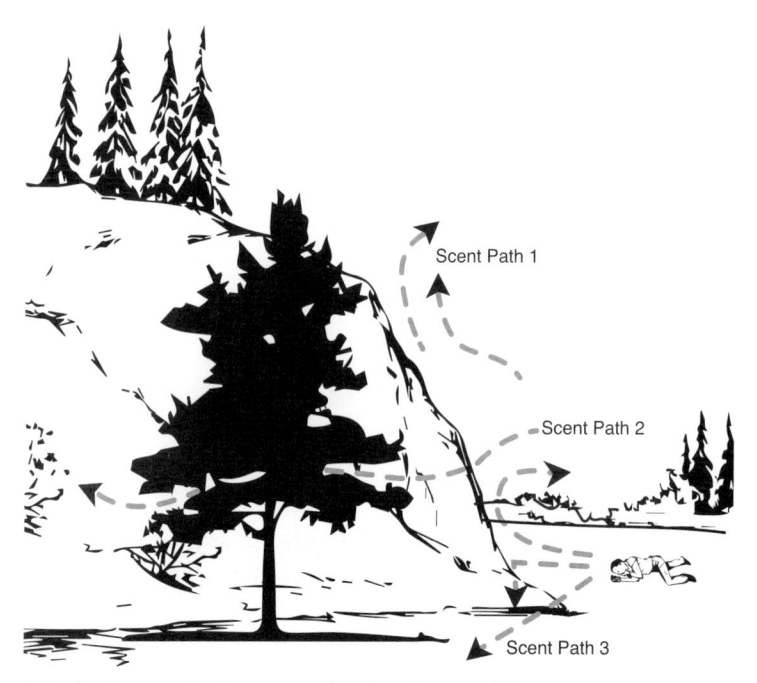

A.9 In this scenario, the scent could follow three possible routes.

above the cliff to collect by the tree. Scent Path 2 is alongside the cliff, going over vegetation, and possibly coming back down to the dog's nose level a distance from its original path. Scent Path 3 shows that scent can travel in any direction after it hits the bottom of the cliff. As always, the path the scent takes depends on the weather and strength of the air currents.

Notes on Scent in Disaster Situations

COLLAPSED STRUCTURES

Working a collapsed structure is entirely different than working in the field or on water. The type of structure, what it is made of, the existence of hot spots from fires, and any other materials or gases that are present will affect the availability of scent. How the structure collapsed will determine where there are air pockets or venting from which your dog can detect scent. Collapsed structures can sometimes cause scent to drift away from the trapped person, just as scent is carried by water.

NATURAL DISASTERS
Natural disasters such as avalanches, mudslides, and earthquakes all have unique scent conditions. Depending on the nature of the disaster, scent may be difficult to locate, or it may take longer to reach the surface where your dog can detect it.

In many cases, dogs use their other senses to find a missing person. For example, a trapped person may call for help, or moan in pain or fear, and dogs can hear and locate the person without using scent.

If the scent travels outside of the disaster area, your dog may pick it up in the same manner that he would in a field situation and follow the scent cone to the source.

Suggested Resources

Bulanda, Susan. *Ready the Training of the Search and Rescue Dog*. Freehold, NJ: Kennel Club Pro, 2010.

Button, Lue. *Practical Scent Dog Training*. Loveland, CO: Alpine Publications, 1990.

Gerritsen, Resi, and Ruud Haak. *K9 Scent Training: A Manual for Training Your Identification, Tracking and Detection Dog*. Calgary: Brush Education, 2015.

———. *K9 Search and Rescue: A Manual for Training the Natural Way*. Calgary: Brush Education, 2014.

Gorny, Boguslaw P. *Tracking for Search and Rescue Dogs: A Practical Manual for Novice and Advanced Handlers*. Calgary: Brush Education, 2003.

Pearsall, Milo D., and Hugo Verbruggen. *Scent: Training to Track, Search and Rescue*. Loveland, CO: Alpine Publications, 1998.

Tweedie, Jan. *On the Trail: A Practical Guide to the Working of Bloodhound and Other Search and Rescue Dogs*. Loveland, CO: Alpine Publications, 1998.

About the Author

Susan and her husband Larry Bulanda—each with over 20 years in the field—have formed and run two K9 SAR units. They formed Coventry Canine Search and Rescue, and then, when many of their missions involved the local fire department's dive squad, they joined Phoenixville Fire Department, creating and managing the K9 division, Phoenixville FDK9SAR.

Susan started her career as a dog trainer when she was very young, and by the time she entered high school had established a business training dogs. She was recognized locally for her accomplishments by 1963 and went on to specialize in problem dogs, experimenting with ways to train dogs using positive reinforcement. She earned a bachelor of arts in Psychology and a master of arts in Education.

In her career, she has trained dogs for hunting, personal protection, drug detection, sled-dog racing (she owned a team of Siberian huskies), trick dog training, and SAR. She is a Certified Animal Behavior Consultant with the International Association of Animal Behavior Consultants (IAABC).

Susan was an adjunct professor for Kutztown University and is an adjunct professor for Carroll Community College, where she teaches courses on dog and cat behavior and a certificate program for students wishing to become dog trainers or behavior consultants.

She is a retired senior conformation judge for the United Kennel Club, was awarded the George Washington Medal of Honor for SAR work, holds a patent for the training and use of toxic mold detection dogs, was a judge twice for England's SAR competitions, and has written seven books, some of which have won national awards. Susan was also instrumental in forming the North American Beauceron Club and is a founding member and newsletter contributor for the National Search Dog Alliance. She continues to help SAR dog handlers worldwide with their training issues.

In the corporate world, Susan was a systems analyst specializing in critical methodologies, production, and inventory control.

K9 Professional Training Series

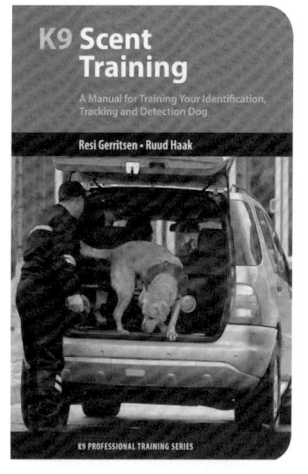

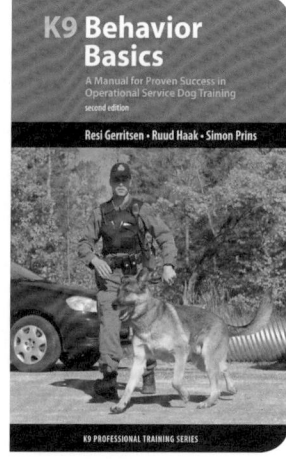

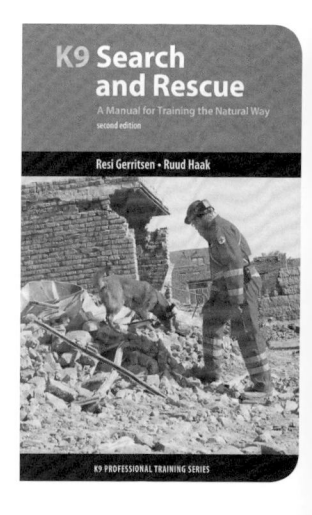

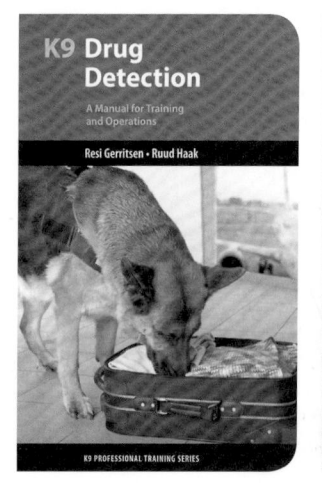

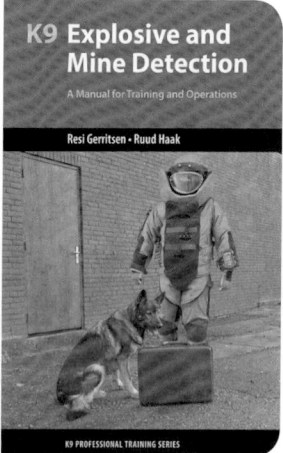

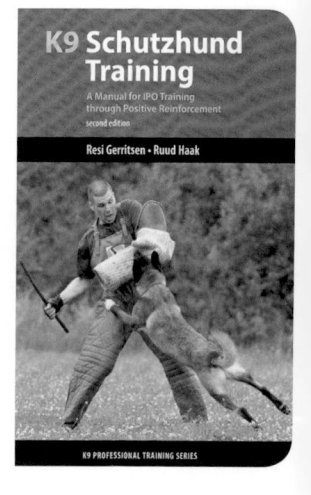

See the complete list at
dogtrainingpress.com